ANTICIPATE THE WORLD YOU WANT

LEARNING FOR ALTERNATIVE FUTURES

MARSHA LYNNE RHEA

ScarecrowEducation
Lanham, Maryland • Toronto • Oxford
2005

Published in the United States of America
by ScarecrowEducation
An imprint of The Rowman & Littlefield Publishing Group, Inc.
4501 Forbes Boulevard, Suite 200, Lanham, Maryland 20706
www.scarecroweducation.com

PO Box 317
Oxford
OX2 9RU, UK

British Library Cataloguing in Publication Information Available

Library of Congress Cataloging-in-Publication Data

Rhea, Marsha Lynne, 1954–
  Anticipate the world you want : learning for alternative futures / Marsha Lynne Rhea.
    p. cm.
  Includes bibliographical references.
  ISBN 1-57886-258-2 (pbk. : alk. paper)
  1. Education—Forecasting. 2. Self-realization. 3. Twenty-first century—Forecasts. 4.
Motivation in education. 5. Expectation (Psychology) I. Title.

  LB41.5.R46 2005
  370.15'23—dc22

                                                                    2005008811

♾™ The paper used in this publication meets the minimum requirements of
American National Standard for Information Sciences—Permanence of Paper
for Printed Library Materials, ANSI/NISO Z39.48-1992.
Manufactured in the United States of America.

CONTENTS

FOREWORD

In recent years most people have been swept up in waves of rapid change and new challenges, but recently we have all experienced totally unexpected, world-shaking crises. Some of these such as global warfare, terrorism, and environmental degradation are man-made; others such as hurricanes, earthquakes, and tsunamis are natural disasters. Responses to all these crises should be made responsibly, with knowledge, intelligence, compassion, and high ethical standards. There may be no time for learning new skills except on the job, no time for determining how to make wise decisions and solve complex problems, and no time for learning how to work both independently and collaboratively.

How do we prepare our young people to deal with such challenges? What kinds of learning are now essential? Despite the fact that every other social institution has evolved dramatically in the last hundred years, educational systems have been remarkably effective at maintaining the status quo. That is what they were planned to do. There may now be, however, a mandate for anticipatory learning, the topic of this insightful book on learning for our time and the future.

Marsha Rhea, in her work as a senior futurist for the Institute for Alternative Futures, specializes in helping many different kinds of organizations to create "preferred futures." No organizations need this more than those responsible for educating the future citizens of our country and inhabitants of an interdependent world. Rhea offers useful guidelines for helping educators to understand that the mastery of basic skills is just the starting point of preparing students for the future and for "split-second opportunities and threats." Although knowledge of the past is essential for understanding the present, she notes, "If learning outcomes look to the past too much, what becomes important is mastering a body of knowledge. When learning faces forward, knowledge becomes a force field flowing into new possibilities."

In my work I have visited numerous schools that are applying new understandings of how best to educate increasingly diverse groups of students. Most of the teachers know that the human brain has enormous plasticity, changing structurally and functionally as a result of learning and experience. This awareness can change their whole approach to teaching and learning. They understand that intelligence too has plasticity and is not a static structure but an open dynamic system that can continue to develop throughout life. They are learning how to facilitate this development by creating environments that are positive, nurturing, and stimulating, and that encourage action and interaction. They understand how to help students to recognize and use their unique strengths and abilities, rather than focusing primarily on "fixing up what's wrong."

Successful teachers know that as new information becomes available, their students must understand how to learn, unlearn, and relearn, and that they must provide the tools to do so. Teachers can catalyze curiosity and keep it alive by giving students meaningful choices and can encourage them to pursue their interests. They model and help them to develop altruism and compassion, and learn to use higher-order thinking skills, including reflection, analysis, synthesis, decision making, and creative problem solving. Rhea points out that "the learning curve for humanity is always an upward spiral. Anticipatory learning provides a solid footing for the climb to a preferred future."

Rhea does not suggest that anticipatory learning be taught as a separate subject but rather that it be integrated throughout the curriculum as a context for learning. Her book offers strategies that not only foster the fuller development of human capacities but also suggest how students can put them to use in positions of leadership as well as in being cooperative, productive members of a group. She points out that many opportunities to develop these skills are offered through community service projects and other local and international activities that allow students to try out newly discovered intelligences and abilities. These opportunities help them to better understand themselves, other people, and other cultures. Rhea notes that the Earth Charter discussed in her book is being used in many schools as an inspiring vehicle for engaging young learners to think positively and creatively about their futures.

Because of the current pressure for raising test scores, many teachers have abandoned some of the most effective ways of helping many children to learn and remain interested in learning. The visual arts, music, dance, and drama provide such tools for learning, as well as engaging the emotions, stirring the imagination, and plumbing the depths of the human spirit. Also, students can practice new ways of communicating, explore a universe of knowledge and ideas, and learn to see patterns and webs of connections through using innovative technologies. Skills such as these, skills that are offered in this book, are essential for our time and the future.

Positive changes are being made in thousands of classrooms and hundreds of schools, but as yet in no whole educational systems. Perhaps some of the farsighted ideas in his book may provide the impetus for whole system change. It is late, but not too late to prepare our young people to deal with the problems that their ancestors have created in the environment, social and political institutions, and the economy. Appropriate educational opportunities can help these young people to create preferred futures for themselves and for humanity.

Dee Dickinson
Chief Learning Officer
New Horizons for Learning
www.newhorizons.org

PREFACE

I have been interested in organizational learning for many years. When I first became a futurist, I was immediately struck by how strategic futuring has more to do with learning than decision making. People have to change the way they think about the future before they can make the kinds of decisions that will transform their organizations.

A favorite saying among futurists is that while you cannot predict the future, you can create it. Anticipatory learning is born out of this belief. We can actually learn how to create our future. If so, schools are a great place to start preparing society to learn its way to a preferred future.

I am not an educator, so I will not presume to offer a new pedagogy. I do offer a fresh look at learning from the perspective of a futurist. I tried to answer one question throughout this work: What would learning look like if it were oriented toward the future? To answer this question, I borrowed ideas and methodologies from many disciplines and adapted them for a school learning environment.

When I wrote about experimentation and rapid prototyping in the chapter on innovation, I laughed out loud in recognition of how aptly I had described what I am doing in writing this book. I am experimenting with lots of ideas, and my framework for anticipatory learning is basically a rapid prototype to make my learning and thinking transparent.

You are now invited to improve on this prototype. Let me know what methodologies and learning practices you would include in anticipatory learning, which ideas are great in theory but simply tough to execute, or which ideas return the best results for your students. I conclude the foresight, identity, direction-setting, and innovation chapters with open questions to educators. There are sure to be more.

I am offering Anticipatory Learning Version 1.0 in the spirit of open-source research. I fully expect that through collaboration we will find the version that will make a significant contribution to a preferred future.

ACKNOWLEDGMENTS

I want to thank Cindy Tursman of ScarecrowEducation for thinking that my ideas in a magazine article had the potential to become this book. She tempted me into a great period of disciplined learning and thinking that will continue to benefit my work as a futurist.

I owe a large debt of gratitude to my colleagues at the Institute for Alternative Futures. I became a futurist because then-IAF Research Director Robert Olson told me I think like a futurist and should consider becoming one. IAF president and founder Clem Bezold's idealism about preferred futures emboldened me to think about what this kind of possibility thinking could mean in education. I thank Jonathan Peck for pulling me into tough projects well outside my knowledge base that forced me to become a better learner. I thank Bill Rowley for his uncommon good sense in telling me I would be crazy not to accept this invitation to write a book. Our interns tell us what impresses them most about IAF is how everyone sits down to lunch together. We are like a family.

I was able to write this book because I could draw upon the work of many futurists and learning experts who have ventured into these questions before me. They are credited in the bibliography. I particularly want to thank Richard Slaughter and Sohail Inayatullah for sharing their extensive writing about future studies. They are original thinkers who deserve more recognition in the United States.

I saved the last acknowledgement for my husband, David Pace. I would have abandoned this undertaking but for all the many daily ways he made it possible for me focus on writing. All too often, people have a vision but lose heart before they implement it. David would not let me do that.

1

A FRAMEWORK FOR ORIENTING LEARNING TO THE FUTURE

Popular expectations about the future fall into one of three categories: more of the same, the sky is falling, or utopia is coming.

Dial back the years to 1999 and think forward to today. Whether we consider events and issues on a global or national scale, or think about our families and ourselves, we did not get more of the same. We are far from the world of 1999.

Believing the sky is falling can prove to be a useful expectation, if we can learn as Chicken Little did in the children's story. After acorns fell on her head, Chicken Little ventured out bravely to tell the king about impending disaster. After a few mishaps, she learned to use an umbrella to protect herself from falling acorns.

Believing that utopia might be possible can inspire us to heroic feats. Atlas in Greek mythology got stuck with the job of holding up the sky and earth. Zeus might have intended this as a punishment, but Atlas' responsibility became a mythic symbol of strength and endurance. He is credited with such marvelous feats as figuring out astronomy and being king of legendary Atlantis.

Recognizing that the world does not stay the same, we have to learn to live in alternative futures. What we need to learn could be simply as pragmatic as knowing when to use an umbrella or as heroic as shouldering the weight of the world.

FRAMING NEW POSSIBILITIES FOR LEARNING

Anticipatory learning is a framework for acquiring the knowledge and skills to understand future possibilities and the ability to collaborate in creating a preferred future. Anticipatory learning involves cycles of discovery, integration, and renewal that keep people and organizations thinking forward in an evolving world. If learning outcomes look to the past too much, what becomes important is mastering a body of knowledge. When learning faces forward, knowledge becomes a force field flowing into new possibilities.

Anticipatory learning organizes in one framework the wisdom, methodologies, and practices that many innovative educators will recognize. Students and educators become collaborators in learning that:

- Explores socially constructed knowledge and insights about alternative futures along a learning continuum of past, present, and future
- Respects and integrates multiple disciplines and different ways of knowing into greater understanding and performance
- Generates new thinking that leaps over present problems and limitations

Schools are a logical laboratory for learning together how to face challenges at a scale and complexity we have never seen before. As one education professor has written about the role of education in the evolution of society, "The future of the world resides in the youth of today. Education's work is to foster a critical citizenry that embraces its responsibility for creating a better world, safe from terrorism and violence, a world defined by freedom and peace" (Jenlink, 2004, p. 65).

The learning curve for humanity is always an upward spiral. Anticipatory learning provides a solid footing for the climb to a preferred future.

FOUR DEFINING DIMENSIONS
OF ANTICIPATORY LEARNING

Anticipatory learning creates a safe space for asking provocative questions and sharing knowledge and opinions about critical issues. This learning discipline has four dimensions: foresight, identity, direction setting, and innovation (see Table 1.1).

Table 1.1. Learning by Exploring, Learning by Doing

Learning by Exploring		Learning by Doing	
Foresight	Identity	Direction Setting	Innovation
		Methodologies	
Orienting in time	Using metaphors as clues	Appreciating prior learning	Unlearning past successes and limitations
Exploring images of the future	Stating intent through values	Framing learning through strategic conversation	Brainstorming the possibilities
Scanning the environment for trends, issues, and developments	Probing the layers of sense making	Defining strategic issues for future focus	Integrating learning across disciplines
Forecasting key drivers of change	Encountering alternative cultures	Expressing personal legacies	Simulating the choices
Brainstorming wild card events	Cultivating multiple dimensions of intelligence	Visioning for great learning and doing	Experimenting and rapid prototyping
Creating scenarios to explore alternative futures	Maximizing different preferences for learning	Setting audacious goals to push ahead	Experiencing the context
	Clarifying personality preferences	Planning a course of action	Continuously evaluating outcomes
	Developing emotional intelligence		

(continued)

Table 1.1. Learning by Exploring, Learning by Doing (*continued*)

Learning by Exploring			Learning by Doing
Foresight	*Identity*	*Direction Setting*	*Innovation*
Practices for Learners			
Placing learning on a developmental timeline	Reflecting on reality	Building trust to promote learning	Seeking creative environments
Bringing images of the future into focus	Listening together	Clarifying roles within the group	Cultivating multiple intelligences
Exploring forecasts and implications for key drivers	Shifting our locus of control	Establishing rules and group norms that work	Abandoning past success
Scanning beyond the textbook version	Seeking wholeness through religion and spirituality	Escaping victim of circumstances beliefs	Risking failure
Exercising the imagination through scenarios			
Practices for Leaders			
Taking inventory of learning needs	Honoring inclusivity of diverse identities	Working with the emotion and energy of visions	Breaking the hold of bureaucracy
Understanding push, pull, and weight	Using storytelling to build shared identity	Gauging different interests within the group	Issuing grand challenges
Outsmarting the forecasts	Debunking limiting myths	Getting out of the way	
Rejecting the official future as reality	Changing minds through multiple formats	Communicating visions until they come true	

Foresight

The foresight dimension analyzes *what we need to know about alternative futures*. The future is not predetermined. It is shaped by countless events, conditions, and choices. The methodologies of foresight make learners aware of what the future will require of them. These methodologies include orienting in time, exploring future images, environmental scanning, forecasting, brainstorming wild cards, and scenario development.

Identity

The identity dimension examines *what we believe about the world and ourselves*. We cannot understand future possibilities or collaborate in creating preferred futures until we grasp how much of what we see today and expect tomorrow comes from inside us. Our mental models shape our thinking and evolution as individuals, organizations, or societies. What we learn and do is bounded by our values, beliefs, emotions, and intelligences. If our identity is bound in a set of beliefs that is no longer useful, we need to adapt to new ways of thinking about ourselves and our world. The methodologies of identity include using metaphors, values, alternative cultures, multiple intelligences, learning style and personality preferences, and emotional intelligence.

Direction Setting

The direction-setting dimension forges the learning of foresight and identity into decisions about *what we want to create in the future and how we will do it*. We use personal reflection and strategic conversations to define our vision for the future. Then we choose goals and actions that will organize our efforts into making this preferred future happen. Collaboration gives us the capacity to take on difficult challenges at any level from individual to global. When direction setting becomes as much about learning as it is about decision making, visions come to life. The methodologies of direction setting are appreciating prior learning, defining strategic issues, visioning, audacious goals, and action planning.

Innovation

The innovation dimension explores the *solutions we can create together*. What innovations are required to achieve our preferred future? Improvements and breakthroughs emerge from processes of creative, cross-disciplinary learning. Innovation practices and techniques that increase the quantity and quality of ideas are like calisthenics for the mind and spirit. The methodologies of innovation are unlearning, brainstorming, multidisciplinary learning, simulations, experiencing the context, and evaluation.

WHAT TO EXPECT IN EACH CHAPTER

The next chapter explores why anticipatory learning is becoming more important in times of rapid change. Progressive educators, businesses, and leaders concerned about global society are calling for a different approach to learning. Anticipatory learning is an attempt to meet this need.

Chapters on each dimension of anticipatory learning follow. In chapter 3, the methodologies of foresight are ordered as they might logically flow in a process of learning. Since learning can be far more organic and dynamic than any step-by-step process, this sequence should not be considered an absolute sequence. Chapter 4 presents the methodologies of identity as windows into either collective or individual identity. The use of windows is a carefully chosen metaphor, because this chapter offers only a brief view into a very complex subject. Foresight and identity are the "learning by exploring" dimensions of anticipatory learning.

Direction setting and innovation are the "learning by doing" dimensions of anticipatory learning. In Chapter 5, on direction setting, the methodologies are ordered to maximize the learning that precedes deciding what to do. The methodologies of innovation described in Chapter 6 are presented as a portfolio of options that can be adopted in any order or combination.

The final chapter imagines the learning required for a visionary future. This chapter opens the door to the possibilities of a better world, an almost utopia, and concludes that education holds the key to this preferred future.

As a framework, anticipatory learning assembles and repurposes several strategic disciplines and applies them to learning. The foresight and direction-setting dimensions draw on the rich legacy of knowledge and practice found in *futures studies*, the term preferred by academics who want to claim a place in the social sciences. Futurists working with clients prefer emphasizing thinking and doing rather than study, so they call this discipline *futuring* or *strategic futuring* to differentiate it from strategic planning.

Many disciplines focus on understanding identity, including psychology, philosophy, sociology, anthropology, spirituality, and religion. Useful elements are borrowed into anticipatory learning. Understanding identity is both ancient and ongoing, and this book is a reminder that we need to honor this dimension.

The theories and methodologies described for innovation come from the disciplines of organizational learning, creativity, and innovation. Businesses have invested heavily in creating these capacities in their workforce. This book connects these disciplines with an exploration of the future, deeper understanding about our identity, and our vision of what to create.

Each chapter on a dimension also features practices for learners and leaders. These are habits of learning or behavior that foster anticipatory learning. The practices for learners may be of greatest interest to students and teachers, and the practices for leaders may be of greatest interest to school administrators and school board members. However, a fundamental tenet of anticipatory learning is our mutual responsibility and accountability for the future. Education professor Raymond Horn (2004) is correct when he posits that any arbitrary lines drawn between learners and leaders stand in the way of our evolution: "The boundaries between administrators, teachers and students need to be blurred. All must participate to some degree in teaching, learning and maintaining the school" (p. 180).

Anticipatory learning is a new framework and this leaves many open questions. Some of these are identified in the dimension chapters. Finally, each of Chapters 2 through 6 concludes with a section for recommended resources. These resources include examples and referrals to organizations with relevant information.

ENGAGING EVERYONE IN ANTICIPATORY LEARNING

Anticipatory learning can take place anywhere and in any course of study. All that is required are minds focused on the future and open to challenging assumptions and thinking creatively about options.

Schools are much more confident about educating about the exterior world than helping explore our interior world. It is more challenging to move from the objective to the subjective. This could make foresight and innovation easier dimensions to adopt in public schools than the study of identity, which takes intimacy, candor, and tolerance for ambiguity. That said, attempting a little learning about identity is far better than pretending that reality is exclusively "out there."

Direction setting is about empowerment. Teaching people how to take charge of their own learning creates the expectation that they can exercise more control over their own destiny. Anticipatory learning takes direction setting out of the exclusive domain of school boards, superintendents, and principals and puts it in the hands of everyone as a better way to focus learning. As learners mature, they should

> become increasingly responsible for their own learning, for making decisions day-to-day as well as for the future. If we accept the notion that the future is too important to leave to chance, the knowledge, skills and tendencies for thinking ahead, for considering, designing and planning for possible futures are essential for young learners. (Jenks, 2004, p. 214)

Anticipatory learning is a framework that applies equally well to how young students learn as it does to how school system leaders learn how to govern wisely. We each have the opportunity to help shape the future. Anticipatory learning prepares us to take this opportunity as seriously as we should.

2

THE PRIORITY FOR LEARNING TO LIVE IN RAPID CHANGE

People agree that a rapid rate of change defines our lives in the 21st century, yet we approach learning as if we have all the time in the world to respond.

In 1970 futurist Alvin Toffler aptly named this phenomenon of rapid change "future shock" in a best-selling book that brought popular attention to thinking about the future. Today futurists delight in demonstrating change acceleration graphs that abruptly jump from gently upward lines to a steep vertical leap. Somewhere up these gravity-defying climbs will be the singularity, a hypothetical point in time where people's imaginations will simply fail to grasp the scope of technological and evolutionary change.

We just need to get over fretting about all this change and do something about learning to live in an era of split-second opportunity and threat. Anticipatory learning is the responsible approach to a future that needs our full attention. Schools have a key role to play in preparing learners of every age for the future. A growing awareness of what the future requires is prompting forward thinkers in education, business, and society to call for a different approach to learning.

EDUCATION LEADERS IDENTIFY THE NEED FOR CHANGE

Schools have always served as a bridge between the knowledge of the past and the learning needed for the future. What is in question today is how well schools, colleges, universities, and even sources of lifelong learning are doing in helping learners anticipate and shape the future. Are schools preparing students for careers that will not exist in their current form and practice? Are university professors and their institutions aiming their incredible capacities in research and development at the world as it was or as it will be? Education leaders who have paused from the daily press of events to reflect on the priorities in education are calling for realignment.

This assessment can be found in the Organisation for Economic Cooperation and Development's (OECD) Schooling for Tomorrow project. This project, which features a set of six scenarios and related research, is a comprehensive and global perspective about the alternatives ahead for education. One of the expert contributors said schools have a "duty to respond flexibly to change, with the courage to grasp accurately and speedily the implications" of a number of pressing global issues (van Aalst, 2001, p. 169).

Expectations for Schooling

In the OECD project, the French inspector general of education named four expectations for schools. Two expectations identify a need for the type of learning encompassed in anticipatory learning: (1) schools should "prepare students from an early age to accept change and the continuous questioning of what was once taken for granted in everyday life. This is not straightforward as all of us need constants to fall back on," and (2) students also should be prepared "to question the results of change—rather than regard it as an end of itself—and to review science and technology critically in terms of their ethical and practical implications for the future" (OECD, 2001, p. 212).

In a futures project on the teaching profession related to this OECD effort, the Ontario (Canada) Ministry of Education (2004) observed:

> The challenges education systems face in the years to come are increasingly complex. A rapidly expanding knowledge base, dramatic advances in information technology, changing job markets and socio-economic disparities in many societies illustrate some of the direct pressures affecting education and its delivery. Broad societal issues such as globalization, environmental concerns, and international security also have an indirect impact on the worldwide delivery of education. (p. 4)

High-Order Skills and Knowledge

Knowledge-based economies require high-order skills and knowledge. New technologies for knowledge management and just-in-time learning make "fixed and pre-determined learning virtually useless . . . instead of 'know-what' (facts and figures) or even 'know-how,' it is 'know-why' that emerges as the most critical skill set for adults to have" (Hodgins, 2000, p. 23). In his assessment of the future for the National Governors Association and the American Society of Training and Development, Hodgins says the new basic skills are innovation, problem solving, creativity, analysis, diagnostics, planning, and the ability to capture and articulate the results of knowledge work with others.

A similar list from Bleedorn (2003) includes what she calls "quality-thinking processes": transformational thinking, global awareness, systemic thinking, recognizing relationships, visionary futuristic thinking, intuitive and paradoxical thought, and critical thinking (p. xi). In the Schooling for Tomorrow project, the OECD (2001) asks "how well school systems in OECD countries really do develop the more general, critical higher-order competencies that are horizontal across subjects and disciplines, building capacity in the young to become informed and responsible in the world of the 21st century" (p. 40).

BUSINESSES SHIFT PRIORITIES
TO NEW SOURCES OF VALUE

Historically the realignment of priorities in U.S. public schools lags behind business by a decade or more. Businesses were well up the adoption curve with computers before schools scrambled to purchase them and train teachers to incorporate computing in classrooms. Schools lag most businesses in the sophisticated application of computer technology.

A case can be made that standards-based reform, now in full momentum under President Bush's No Child Left Behind act, is a crude attempt at quality improvement processes to achieve greater accountability. In the 1980s and 1990s, thousands of businesses took their processes apart and rebuilt them from the ground up for the precision and productivity they needed to

compete against rising quality standards. Workers had to get the basics precisely right. Today students are also expected to get the basics right, and the
drilling that went into process improvement in business is now going into
testing in schools.

Now that most businesses have addressed quality, they are turning to
three new sources of strategic advantage: collaboration, organizational learning, and innovation. They want employees skilled at working in project
teams, strategic alliances, and outsourcing up and down the value chain.
They want employees adept at connecting to corporate knowledge and
building new capabilities in a knowledge economy. They want to escape the
downward pressure on prices through innovation. Employers already are in-
vesting in training and development to acquire these new skills as they try to
stay one step ahead of marketplace requirements. Schools and universities
will soon be playing catch-up to this marketplace imperative for collaboration, organizational learning, and innovation.

Collaboration in Complex Projects

With greater connectivity, companies are able to maximize their options for
getting work done. They can rely on a more flexible network of human resources within and beyond their organization. They can take on more complex projects, because they can coordinate an interdependent team of talent.
They can merge the knowledge and expertise of different disciplines to create new insights. They can turn on the power of many, if they have individuals who know how to work well together.

Organizational Learning for Rapid Change

Employers have a growing need for employees who can learn new skills or
knowledge in response to rapid change and new opportunities. In a knowledge economy, businesses and individuals have to know how to learn and re-
member what they know. Since many of the problems businesses need to
solve in a complex world are new challenges, they need people with an ability to leap from the known into the unknown with confidence.

Innovation in Business

The return on creativity and innovation is obvious in fields like technology, science, and entertainment, but it is no less valuable in manufacturing and service businesses. When most companies can compete on price and value, the game goes to the innovator. Value differentiation is increasingly in the services that surround a product. Disruptive innovations defy categories and mix ideas and tools in surprising ways. Employers need employees who are eager to think outside the book they studied in school.

SOCIETY REQUIRES ANTICIPATORY LEARNING

H. G. Wells was not overstating the case when he said, "human history becomes more and more a race between education and catastrophe." Futurist Richard Slaughter (2003), quoted by the BBC on skills we will need for the future, shares this conviction: "Our species is challenged to learn the arts of planet management—to learn them fast. The difficulty is: there's no rulebook. So we are challenged to evolve, grow, take responsibility, learn to operate on a global scale, but sensitively, carefully and with a very clear opening to the long view" (p. 2).

According to Gidley's (2004) review of the research on young people's future views:

> young people sense a spiritual vacuum in their society (though only some are able to articulate it). They are deeply concerned about what they see as a lack of values and ethics in politics and the corporate business world. Young people are idealistic when given a chance to express themselves. They want a clean, green world with ethics and meaning, a world where everyone is treated fairly. They want work that is meaningful and where they are treated with respect and valued. (p. 20)

What the research showed is that their future will be "full of their fears" unless they are given the knowledge and skills to create their preferred future (Gidley, 2004, p. 20).

The conviction that anticipatory learning is essential to our future first appeared in "No Limits to Learning," a 1979 report to the Club of Rome. This treatise for global sustainability and well-being states:

> Anticipation is the capacity to face new, possibly unprecedented, situations; it is the acid test for innovative learning processes. Anticipation is the ability to deal with the future, to foresee coming events as well as to evaluate the medium-term and long-range consequences of current decisions and actions. It requires not only learning from experience but also "experiencing" vicarious or envisioned situations. An especially important feature of anticipation is the capacity to account for unintended side effects, or "surprise effects" as some people call them. Furthermore, anticipation is not limited simply to encouraging desirable trends and averting potentially catastrophic ones: it is also the "inventing" or creating of new alternatives where none existed before. (Botkin, Elmandjra, & Malitza, 1979, p. 44)

Despite this eloquent case more than 20 years ago, few people today recognize anticipatory learning as a global priority. Futurist Sohail Inayatullah (2003) identified six reasons thinking about the future should be part of what he calls anticipatory action learning. The benefits he identified apply equally well to the practices and methods of anticipatory learning described in this book:

- To make better decisions. For governments this may be to meet the changing needs of citizens. For businesses it may be for greater profit or success on the triple bottom line of property, social justice, and environment. For school boards it may be authorizing investments in new facilities or instructional approaches.
- Learning about new ideas and methods to increase the knowledge of students, employees, managers, and directors.
- Learning how to learn and develop individual and organizational potential. The goal is to empower, enabling people to take charge of their future.
- Finding new memes (social genes) and finding ways to have organizations select them and make them real (for example: just-in-time learning, lifelong learning, and even No Child Left Behind for all its surrounding controversy in the United States).
- Using emergence for qualitative transformation by moving an organization to the edge of chaos for new ideas that can push a system to a qualitative shift.

- Changing who we are at the spiritual level of our inner lives as individuals as well as the organization's inner life.

"It is thus more than learning to learn; it is about learning and healing, individual and collective, inner and external" (Inayatullah, 2003, p. 36).

$e \frown$

RECOMMENDED RESOURCES

2020 Scenarios for Schooling Illustrate Alternative Futures

The Organisation for Economic Co-operation and Development (OECD) commissioned a set of six scenarios for schooling looking ahead to 2020. This perspective illustrates how major forces apart from national priorities and politics are shaping the options for schools in more affluent nations like the United States. The scenario abstracts below give the broad outlines of what schools would be like in each alternative future, and I have assigned priority ratings to each. The OECD Schooling for Tomorrow project makes an implicit case for the learning processes that are characterized in this book as anticipatory learning. Four of the six scenarios describe alternative futures in which anticipatory learning would be a high priority. For more information on this project and to read the full scenarios and other commentary, visit the OECD website at www.oecd.org.

Scenario 1.a: "Bureaucratic School Systems Continue"

Low Priority for Anticipatory Learning: This scenario is built on the continuation of powerfully bureaucratic systems, strong pressures toward uniformity, and resistance to radical change. Curriculum and qualifications are central areas of policy, and student assessments are key elements of accountability, though questions persist over how far to develop capacities to learn. Individual classroom and teacher models remain dominant.

Scenario 1.b: "Teacher Exodus—the 'Meltdown Scenario'"

Medium Priority for Anticipatory Learning: There would be a major crisis of teacher shortages, highly resistant to conventional policy responses. It is triggered by a rapidly aging profession, exacerbated by low teacher morale and buoyant opportunities in more attractive graduate jobs. Where teacher shortages are acute they have detrimental effects on student learning. Widely different organizational responses to the shortages occur—some traditional, some highly innovative—and possibly include greater use of information communication technologies.

Scenario 2.a: "Schools as Core Social Centers"

High Priority for Anticipatory Learning: The school here enjoys widespread recognition as the most effective bulwark against social, family, and community fragmentation. It is now heavily defined by collective and community tasks. This leads to extensive shared responsibilities between schools and other community bodies, sources of expertise, and institutions of further and continuing education, helping foster high teacher professionalism. The focus of learning broadens with more explicit attention given to non-cognitive outcomes, values and citizenship. A wide range of organizational forms and settings emerge, with strong emphasis on informal learning.

Scenario 2.b: "Schools as Focused Learning Organizations"

High Priority for Anticipatory Learning: Schools are revitalized around a strong knowledge rather than social agenda, in a culture of high quality, experimentation, diversity, and innovation. New forms of evaluation and competence assessment flourish. Information communication technologies are used extensively alongside other learning media, traditional and new. Knowledge management comes to the fore, and a very large majority of schools justify the label "learning organizations" with extensive links to tertiary education and other diverse organizations. Flourishing research on pedagogy and the science of learning is systematically applied.

Scenario 3.a: "Learning Networks and the Network Society"

High Priority for Anticipatory Learning: Dissatisfaction and diversified demand leads to the abandonment of schools in favor of a multitude of learning networks, quickened by the extensive possibilities of powerful, inexpensive information communication technologies. Various cultural, religious, and community voices come to the fore in the socialization and learning arrangements for children, some very local in character, others using distance and cross-border networking. Greater expression is given to learning for different cultures and values through networks of community interests. Small group, homeschooling, and individualized arrangements become widespread.

Scenario 3.b: "Extending the Market Model"

High Priority for Anticipatory Learning: Existing market features in education are significantly extended as governments encourage diversification in a broader environment of market-led change. This is fueled by dissatisfaction by "strategic consumers" in cultures where school is commonly viewed as a private as well as a public good. Many new providers are stimulated to come into the learning market, encouraged by thoroughgoing reforms of funding structures, incentives, and regulation. Flourishing indicators, measures, and accreditation arrangements start to displace direct public monitoring and curriculum regulation. The most valued learning is determined by choices and demands—whether of those buying educational services or of those, such as employers, giving market value to different forms of learning. A strong focus on noncognitive outcomes and values might be expected to emerge.

Creating Preferred Futures Fosters Futures-Oriented Learning

Creating Preferred Futures is an interdisciplinary, facilitated online learning environment created by K–12 teachers for K–12 teachers and their students. The creators of this project advocate blending futures-oriented learning into regular classroom experience. Their philosophy, as conveyed in their statement of belief, conveys the basic principles for anticipatory learning for students of any age.

> We believe the following:
> Children and youth, as well as lifelong learners, need to be able to recognize patterns of change, identify trends, draw implications and create alternative futures scenarios so they will be better equipped to anticipate and plan for future challenges and opportunities.

Learning in a futures-oriented context ought to be informed by the latest research—for example, cooperative learning, diverse learning styles, multiple intelligences, technology, and brain research.

Additional emphasis must be placed on applications, that is, not only being outfitted with facts and knowledge but also being able to place learning in context and then being able to do something productive with that information.

The importance of linear and nonlinear systems in making sense of the world must be woven throughout various disciplines and content areas so students are able to see interrelationships, correlations, interdependencies, and vital connections to their own daily experiences.

In dealing with futures-oriented themes in learning, there comes an added burden on making the learning comprehensible to students (for example, in constructing the rubrics for coursework and activities). That is, until students successfully begin identifying and navigating the connections inherent in a more robust past-present-future learning continuum. Then notice the students taking responsibility for their own learning and running with it.

Learning is enhanced when the learning environment is one in which the Socratic method of critical inquiry and constructivist opportunities for students are present.

The World Wide Web and other technology-based media are powerful tools for learning; however, they must always be viewed and used in context and with appropriate perspective. The human-to-human contact point between the student and a caring, competent facilitator of learning is still the most powerful catalyst for learning and accumulating wisdom. (Creating Preferred Futures, 2005)

To access information on futures methodologies customized for the classroom, go to www.cpfonline.org/cpf/.

Educator David Hicks' Rationale
for a Futures Dimension in the Curriculum

David Hicks has written extensively about using futures in K–12 education. He teaches at Bath Spa University College in the United Kingdom. In a *Journal of Futures Studies* article, he set out these learning outcomes as the rationale for educating about the future:

Pupil Motivation: Public expectation about the future can affect behavior in the present, for example, that something is, or is not, worth working for. Clear images of desired personal goals can help stimulate motivation and achievement.

Anticipating Change: Anticipatory skills and flexibility of mind are important in times of rapid change. Such skills enable pupils to deal more effectively with uncertainty and to initiate rather than merely respond to change.

Critical Thinking: In weighing up information, considering trends, and imagining alternatives, pupils will need to exercise reflective and critical thinking. This is often triggered by realizing the contradictions between how the world is now and how one would like it to be.

Clarifying Values: All images of the future are underpinned by differing value assumptions about human nature and society. In a democratic society, pupils need to be able to begin to identify such value judgments before they can themselves make appropriate choices between alternatives.

Decision Making: Becoming more aware of trends and events that are likely to influence one's future, and investigating the possible consequences of one's actions on others in the future, leads to more thoughtful decision making in the present.

Creative Imagination: One faculty that can contribute to, and that is particularly enhanced by, designing alternative futures is that of creative imagination. Both this and critical thinking are needed to envision a range of preferable futures from the personal to the global.

A Better World: It is important in a democratic society that pupils develop their sense of vision, particularly in relation to more just and sustainable futures. Such forward-looking thinking is an essential ingredient in both preserving and improving society.

Responsible Citizenship: Critical participation in democratic life leads to the development of political skills and thus more active and responsible citizenship. Future generations are then more likely to benefit, rather than lose, from decisions made today. (Hicks, 2003, p. 56–57)

3

LEARNING WITH THE FUTURE IN SIGHT

Learning is an iterative process of adapting and updating our knowledge and skills to meet new requirements and challenges in the future. While we build on what we know, we cannot trust the past to be a reliable guide to what we will need to know. The future is not simply a bigger and better version of the past.

Many things will change. Things that should not change will and other things that should change will not. Some changes will be breakthroughs or breakdowns that push us into new possibilities. Foresight is the dimension of anticipatory learning that attempts to make sense of this changing world.

Foresight is thinking ahead to how trends, issues, and developments that can be observed in the present are likely to shape alternative futures. Foresight helps answer these questions:

- What are the key forces that are shaping the future?
- What might be their possible outcomes?
- What implications could they have for the learning and actions that must happen in the present?

WHY CHANGE HAPPENS

Technology as a Force of Change

We need a better understanding of how change happens to begin answering these questions about the future. Dator (2002) got many explanations for why change happens when he asked teachers of futures studies around the world to describe their theories of social change. His own answer is: "I have concluded that technology is a major agent of social change, contributing significantly to the creation of all of the other 'tsunamis' (demographics, global environmental change, political-economic instabilities, cultural transformations, etc.) upon which we all must 'surf' (or drown)" (p. 8).

Educators would agree with the importance he places on technological change. The impact of information communication technologies on learning is one of the more profound changes of our time. Writing on a computer is a very different mental process than writing on a piece of paper. Researching on the Web is wider ranging and more creative than flipping through the trusty encyclopedia in the school library. Mathematics and the sciences are transformed by computing capacity. Thanks to networking technologies, homework bears no resemblance to the solo work of yesteryear. A final class project is just as likely to be a video or a website as a written report. And throughout higher education and in many high schools, online learning is the new distance learning.

Evolution as a Force of Change

Others subscribe to an evolutionary theory of change and use a systems view to explain increasing complexity in the world. Evolutionary change is not necessarily steady and incremental. Significant bifurcations can disrupt continuity and bring about transformation. Just as living organisms sense their changing environment and adapt, living systems are capable of sensing new challenges and reorganizing to meet them.

This chapter opens with an evolutionary explanation of learning as adaptation and growth. When people describe how schools must change from an industrial economy model to one that fits a knowledge-based economy, they are describing evolutionary change. Another important evolution in schools has been meeting the special needs of diverse populations. The next logical step in this evolutionary march could be personal learning plans for every student.

Social Choice as a Force of Change

Sociologist and futurist Wendell Bell (2002) says:

> any adequate theory of society and social change . . . must include people . . . as active, purposeful, responsible and creative beings whose future-oriented behavior has consequences for their own lives and for social structures and cultures. Such people may be only partially informed, often misinformed, calculating but sometimes wrong in their calculations, occasionally have fuzzy goals that are only partially consistent with each other, subject to social and cultural pressures, and often too fixated on the short range. Nonetheless, they are accountable for their actions, all of which is precisely why, whether they are top leaders or ordinary people, they often need help in making right choices and taking effective actions. (p. 37–38)

A whole host of education initiatives can be traced to this conviction that people must be prepared to make social choices as responsible citizens. Basic skills education, citizenship education, American history and government, character education, health education, sex education, and environmental education are all attempts to teach students to make wise choices in areas of great consequence to society. Schools face a growing and urgent list of challenges to help prepare responsible and creative citizens. It includes globalization, sustainability, security, economic disparity, ethics, and health and wellness.

Dynamics of Change

To understand change, we also need to consider what futurist Inayatullah (2000) calls the dynamics of push, pull, and weight. Push comes from external forces like new technologies, demographic changes, and economic transitions. Pull comes from the internal force of a vision or an image of the future. (How images work is explained later in this chapter; vision is explained in Chapter 4.) Weight refers to structures that are difficult to change, like class, hierarchy, religion, and, as many would argue, bureaucracy in schools. Human nature may carry the greatest weight against change.

METHODOLOGIES FOR LEARNING WITH FORESIGHT

Foresight relies on critical thinking processes to see what is happening and to question simple assumptions about what it could mean. Foresight can make learners remarkably aware of what the future will require of them. A statement attributed to science fiction author William Gibson had it right: "The future is here. It is just not widely distributed yet."

Educators can use these methods to help students identify and interpret major forces of change:

- Interpreting patterns and events in history that continue through the present into the future
- Understanding how images of the future, including what people believe to be the "official" future, shape perceptions
- Scanning the environment for trends and emerging issues
- Forecasting how drivers of change could shape the future
- Brainstorming wild card events
- Creating scenarios to explore alternative futures

Orienting in Time

Historians and futurists practice similar disciplines, simply at different places on the continuum of time. The worst travesty in teaching history is not courses and textbooks that stop short of the present; it is teaching history without a belief that conditions and events in the past are a prologue to the future. People are always working out the past in the present. History is not destiny, but it does set important boundaries around what is possible for the future.

Macrohistory studies the histories of social systems in search of patterns of social change. Centuries of conflict in regions and among cultures and religions shape the options people will accept in the present. Even seemingly straightforward decisions in the past, like how a nation develops its infrastructure, are powerful preconditions to what people will do in the future. This country's history of relying on resource extraction to industrialize helps explain the "weight" we now see against adopting resource-conserving strategies.

Exploring Images of the Future

Science fiction literature and movies shape the images students have of the future. These creative works explore what capabilities we may have or what freedoms we may lose. The *Matrix* series and *Minority Report* are recent examples of movies popular with young people. Author Michael Crichton has influenced what people think about nanotechnology with his bestseller *Prey*. Baby boomers and Generation Xers see the distant future through the vision of the *Star Trek* television and movies series or the *Star Wars* movies. These persuasive stories about the future call into question unresolved tensions around technology, science, and the human condition in a compelling way.

Recognizing images of the "official" future can be more difficult, because they hide in plain sight as logical extensions of what most people believe about the present. As Finnish futurist Anita Rubin (2002) explains, "These interpretations reveal the tone of the time and of the reality that people are living through. While the reality of today can be seen as a production of yesterday's choices and decisions, so also the images of the future are the projections of today" (p. 297).

A particularly apt summary of the "official" future for education can be found in the 2004 "Teaching as a Profession" project that involved about 160 people across Ontario thinking about the future of education. This project identified a rapidly expanding knowledge base, dramatic advances in information technology, changing job markets and socioeconomic disparities, globalization, environmental concerns, and international security as factors affecting the future of education (Ontario Ministry of Education, 2004, p. 4).

This "official" future is already affecting important decisions in the education system now. A rapidly expanding knowledge base creates an urgency to accelerate learning. Higher math and science courses are pushed out of high school curriculums and into middle and junior high. Advanced placement courses give students a head start on college. Advances in information technology have pushed computers into every classroom, and some school districts issue them to every student just as textbooks are. School-to-work programs, lifelong learning initiatives, and No Child Left Behind are all expectable responses to a future promising changing job markets and socioeconomic disparities. Students around the globe are engaging in innovative programs using the Internet for environmental and peacemaking projects.

The official future powerfully shapes what and how people learn. Whether we realize it or not, we are all under the power of its influence. Defining the official future is an important step in critical thinking. The validity of this baseline assumption can be tested through additional foresight processes.

Scanning the Environment
for Trends, Issues, and Developments

Environmental scanning is much more than assigning students to find current events related to the subjects they are studying. Scanning is an active process of sense making. A lot happens in a complex world. Sorting through all that is happening to find what will become important in shaping the future is a higher-order thinking skill. Scanning takes an ability to see patterns, correlate relevance, and project possibilities.

Scanning is the search for trends, developments, and emerging issues that can become key drivers of the future. Just like the scientific method, scanning uses an initial hypothesis as a filter for the search. A scanning hypothesis focuses the search for evidence in the present that could lead to specific changes in the future. We might scan social trends with a hypothesis that new initiatives in schools mirror society. We could hypothesize that a new understanding of how the brain works could change how students are taught as we scan developments in brain science. Scanning is an analytical process, but it benefits from a lively intellectual curiosity, intuitive thinking, and a healthy skepticism about the initial hypothesis.

A trend is a pattern of change over time in things of importance to us. Some trends have a high degree of certainty. Schools routinely conduct a census to determine how many children are likely to enter kindergarten at some future date. Universities and colleges look to anticipated high school graduation rates to project potential enrollment. Government census agencies worldwide project how many people their countries will have in ten to twenty years. But demographic projections are not entirely reliable. The United Nations had to revise its population projections to account for declining birthrates worldwide. Cities and schools can underestimate population changes during an economic boom or bust.

Developments involve new capacities or changed conditions. Genetics and sequencing the human genome have changed medicine. The World

Wide Web transformed global communications, knowledge sharing, and entertainment. AIDS is changing the social and economic well-being for several generations to come in many African communities. Wars, droughts, and natural disasters can change conditions in countries and communities. A major employer's decision to relocate can have far-reaching implications for a local community.

Issues arise from a convergence of trends and developments. Globalization is an example. It is the outcome of a set of trends and developments that includes changes in global communications and transportation, markets, cultural patterns, and education.

Trends, developments, and issues that will have a great impact on the future are called key drivers or major forces. Globalization could be an important driver for students, because it enables their future jobs to be located anywhere. Globalization also could bring an influx of economic refugees into the schools. As communities lose jobs offshore, globalization becomes a key driver in their economic future.

Scanning is systematic research. To convey the categories for this search, futurists use an acronym—STEEPV—for social, technological, economic, environmental, political, and values trends. Another simple way to think systematically in scanning is to answer these six questions:

- Who are we becoming?
- What will our world be like?
- How will we learn?
- What capabilities will we have?
- What will organizations become?
- What values will guide us?

Scanners also use time as a frame of reference. Time horizons vary with the nature of the scan. For a student contemplating a career choice, the relevant time horizon could be a near term of 4 to 6 years. For a school system planning to update its curriculum, the time horizon could be more like 10 years. Scholars defining the direction of a discipline or profession may scan out 20 years or more to anticipate what areas of research and development will be needed.

Finding relevant information is not difficult. Evidence of trends, developments, and issues can be found in a multitude of sources. Electronic newsletters provide a steady stream of news and developments into computer mail-boxes. Specialized websites aggregate data, information, and reports. What is more difficult is determining which sources can be trusted. Judging the credibility and validity of sources is another critical thinking skill in antici-patory learning.

For many topics, newspapers and popular magazines can be as useful as journals and research studies. Surveying the person on the street could be a better bellwether of social trends than scanning the written work of expert think tanks. The most informative sources have synthesized a myriad of rel-evant information into a coherent framework. Books remain an invaluable source, even in this era when Google, the name of the popular search engine, is now used as a verb.

Thought leaders are another important source. As longtime observers, they may have highly evolved explanations for how change happens in their field of interest. They also are likely to be working at the edge of current practice and possibilities, and as a consequence they are very influential in setting the course to a preferred future.

Teams are better than individuals at the sense making required in scan-ning. They are able to scan a wider range of sources. As will be explained in the next chapter, teams that have a wide range of experiences, beliefs, and knowledge are the most effective. If a scanning team is not an option, indi-vidual scanners still can test their assumptions against scans done by others. They can participate in communities of practice or interest that are develop-ing new knowledge in their field or area of concern. These communities can be found wherever people gather around a common interest, such as action-learning teams on the job and special groups within nonprofit organizations and associations.

Analyzing Trends and Issues for Implications

Trends, developments, and issues can be analyzed in many ways. How un-certain is the trend? Does an issue have sufficient impact to be considered a key driver? What is the rate of change associated with a trend? What forces may be causing this issue to continue? Will it continue or could some new development alter its course? Is there a life cycle to this issue, before other issues replace it as a priority?

Because our world consists of interconnected and interdependent systems, understanding the implications requires multidimensional thinking. Cross-impact analysis can be used to interpret how trends and developments in one area might interact with other trends. Two basic methods are common:

- A cross-impact analysis matrix arrays trends and issues across the horizontal and vertical axes to systematically compare every trend and issue against each other. The impact that the interaction of each set of two factors could have on the future is examined in either qualitative or quantitative terms. This process can be used to discover which of the trends and issues could be most influential in a dynamic system.
- A futures wheel or implications wheel works like a mind map. One trend or issue is placed at the center, and the different implications associated with it are arrayed around it. To follow the cascade of possible outcomes, these first-order implications can be used to brainstorm second-order implications and so forth until several levels of implications have been considered.

Forecasting Key Drivers of Change

Forecasts are projections of what could happen to a key driver at some future time. These statements are educated guesses based on analyzing the interplay of related trends, issues, and developments. Econometric forecasts use historical patterns to say what will happen in the future. When economists forecast increases in gross national product or cost of living, they are looking at past patterns and tempering their estimates with an awareness of any disruptive forces that could happen. In periods of extreme change, these educated guesses can be quite inaccurate.

Forecasts are useful devices because they start to bound the possibilities for what to anticipate in the future. A forecast might state that by 2012, 60 percent of the U.S. adult population will have some college education. Another 2012 forecast might state that 45 percent of U.S. workers will be in professional and managerial jobs. These forecasts can be extrapolated from current trends in educational attainment and employment to support an overall forecast that the United States is transitioning into a knowledge-based economy.

Forecasts that extrapolate from current trends are relatively safe. Provocative forecasts assume surprising changes. As long as they align with signals of change that can be detected in the present, they can push the edges of plausibility and draw attention to possibilities for dramatic change. A forecast that within a decade textbooks will be replaced by portable and updateable e-books is provocative. However, it is technically feasible, consistent with how some teachers are now using the Web to supplement learning, and an elegant solution for school systems in the face of rising textbook costs. At the right price point, such a device would make issuing and reclaiming textbooks a chore of the past. A provocative forecast could posit how digitized media and hypertext will lead to customized, self-directed learning.

Futurist Wendy Schultz (speech, August 2004) issued such a provocative forecast when she told futurist audiences in the United States and Mexico that by 2048 the last linear thinker will have died. She says our mental structures will change, and we will become geodesic thinkers adept at systems thinking and navigating complexity. Our learning technologies will be hypermedia, ambient intelligence, and oral and visual experiences that can allow our minds to master point-to-multipoint thinking.

Brainstorming Wild-Card Events

Anticipatory learning requires more imagination and creativity than most of us feel we are permitted to exercise. Wild cards are the ultimate permission to think about anything that could happen. They are high-impact, low-probability events that go well beyond what we assume will happen. They may appear far-fetched, but history shows wild cards occasionally occur and have enormous impact. Two examples of wild-card events are the fall of the Berlin Wall and the terrorist attacks of 9-11.

Wild cards are the ultimate "what if" question. What if a major earthquake rocks the center of the United States? What if a major hole opens up in the ozone over Antarctica? What if the United States, Canada, and Mexico unite as one government? What if we experience a widespread spiritual awakening in which we are no longer at odds with one another?

Some wild cards are not all that crazy; they are just far ahead of what we now believe to be possible. What if we are able to cure cancer, Alzheimer's, and AIDS? Someone is asking that question today and taking the long view that what is wild now will be doable in the future. One person's wild card can become another person's lifelong vision.

Creating Scenarios to Explore Alternative Futures

Scenarios are alternative descriptions or stories of how the future might unfold. They are powerful learning tools, because they help us try on different versions of the future. Scenarios can help us achieve strategic perspective, because they often raise fundamental questions about issues and situations we now simply accept. By making explicit deeply held values, they make room for alternative thinking in our worldviews. They help us define our sense of a preferred future, and find the best strategies for making it happen. We can use scenarios in organizations and communities to build understanding and support for new directions and initiatives.

Scenarios are not predictions of the future. They describe how key internal and external trends, issues, and developments could interact in alternative versions of the future. Scenarios present internally consistent images of plausible yet different futures. Scenarios can expand our field of view and help us see possible threats and opportunities that otherwise might remain hidden. Thinking through potential "dark side" scenarios can help us imagine how to turn destructive energy into a force for creating a preferred future. Visionary scenarios sometimes begin with very bad surprises shaking people free from their routine thinking and actions.

A set of four scenarios works best for learning. With only two scenarios, too many possibilities remain unexplored. Three scenarios make a workable set, but people often are tempted to focus on the "moderate middle" scenario and pay less attention to the others. A set of four scenarios has no middle, but it is still a manageable number to explore.

Futurist Clem Bezold (personal communication) pioneered an approach to developing scenarios that uses archetypes to create memorable stories. Of the four scenarios, he intentionally places two in what he calls the zone of high aspirations to give more weight to the possibilities of a preferred future. The four archetypal scenarios are described below.

- The "business as usual" scenario follows conventional expectation about the future and relies on official forecasts and expectable trends.

It is typically a moderately optimistic, continued-growth scenario in which problems remain but prove manageable. Few radical departures occur from current directions and practices. When people rank the likelihood of the four scenarios, this familiar scenario wins.

A "business as usual" scenario for schools might feature steady progress in achieving basic skills while renewing interest in the arts, physical and health education, and science. Money would remain tight as governments shift their priorities to an aging society.

- The "hard times" scenario is a feared future where many of the things that can go wrong do. Organizations, communities, and governments that ignore these possibilities risk being blindsided. This scenario shows how important negative trends and events might play out. The "hard times" scenario does not begin with a single catastrophe. The more plausible plot line is a cascade of events that reaches a tipping point into hard times. It can be set at different levels of severity, from slow growth and worsening problems all the way to economic depression and social collapse.

A "hard times" scenario for schools might feature widespread academic failure, increases in home schooling, withdrawal of public support, severe teacher shortages, and online courses developed in China and successfully marketed globally.

- The "aspirational" scenario is one of the two preferred future scenarios. It explores a significant change to the dominant paradigm operating within an organization or field. Key institutional structures or systems might change, or new business models might succeed in the marketplace. It challenges current assumptions about the external framework of a successful future.

An "aspirational" scenario for schools might describe dismantling the age-bound system and shifting into performance-based progression. Students of all ages would learn at their individualized level in specific academic disciplines. Adults would be just as likely to pursue their lifelong learning in community schools as in colleges and universities.

- The "visionary" scenario imagines people experiencing a change of minds and hearts and coming together to reshape their world. It explores what happens when people agree to create the best future they can imagine. It is mostly a positive scenario, but it may identify new challenges and displacements for some people as different values and priorities define the future.

A "visionary" scenario for schools might have communities so committed to education that they use every resource they have to ensure the success of students. Tutoring, mentoring, and internships might be widely accepted civic responsibilities. Students, teachers, and citizens would move seamlessly from classroom to community-based learning experiences in a system that believes learning should be the focus of everyone's lives.

This sequence of steps is effective in developing scenarios:

1. Determine the learning objectives and audience for the scenarios.
2. Decide what form will serve the objectives and audience best. Some audiences like brief narratives; others may want more quantified data; still others may learn best from graphic images.
3. Clarify the strategic questions about alternative futures that the scenarios should help answer.
4. Choose a period of time to be explored by the scenarios (e.g., 5, 10, or 20 years).
5. Identify key drivers that will shape the future in that time period.
6. Develop and describe forecasts for the key drivers as they might play out in each alternative future.
7. Place these drivers and their forecasts into a scenario matrix to organize the key differences across the set of scenarios. This matrix is useful later as another device for communicating what happens in each scenario.
8. Frame a preliminary description or basic plotline for the four scenarios, considering important outcomes and related implications.
9. Create each scenario with internal coherence and plausibility.
10. Title the scenarios with names that creatively communicate their essence. Using a metaphor convention is a useful device for conveying the nature of each scenario.
11. Field-test the scenarios and refine them if others find they do not have the internal consistency to be plausible accounts of alternative futures.

FORESIGHT PRACTICES FOR LEARNERS

Placing Learning on a Developmental Timeline

Bringing both history and foresight into learning reminds us that what we are learning today fits into a continuum of human understanding. How has the knowledge in any given field progressed? When young children learn to read, they are enacting an ancient skill that was fundamental to moving beyond the limitations of oral culture. The conventions of reading shape the way we learn and how we communicate with one another. For the elementary school student, the future contains multiple possibilities: the ability to read more difficult literature, the opportunity to choose what to read, and even the question of what kind of reading will be important in the future. Reading is much more than mastering letters, words, and concepts of increasing difficulty; we are learning inside a developing story in which we all have a role.

Every area of study has a developmental line. To return to our reading example, an alphabet, libraries, printing presses, and computers all have contributed to the capacity to read. Social trends and values also affect reading. At a different point in history, we did not value teaching everyone to read. Class, race, and gender excluded people. Politics also has a role in this developmental story. Reading has been and can be forbidden if someone in power does not want something read. Imagine explaining this developmental story to children who are learning to read to put their learning in perspective. We can tell similar stories for science, mathematics, literature, geography, psychology, and many other fields of study.

These stories can be illustrated on a timeline with key developments and concepts geared to an age-appropriate level. The objective is to place the current study within the context of human development and learning. These timelines teach an important idea: our learning builds on a past, it is not fixed in the present, and it will change as we confront new demands and opportunities in the future.

Bringing Images of the Future Into Focus

Images of the future represent what we believe will be the outcome of trends and issues we observe in the present. As the next chapter explains, these images are a realization of our hopes, fears, and worldviews. And as the chapter on direction setting further explains, what we believe in will influence what we actually do create. A good way to begin examining these assumptions is to deconstruct images of the future.

The first step is to assemble as many images of the future as possible from literature, movies, television, and other media. Determine what other images the learners themselves may have. If the image of the future is a high-tech wonderland, what trends and developments set the stage for it? How does current science limit this future? What scientific developments might favor it? Would society value a high-tech wonderland or find this image too devoid of high-touch experiences? In what ways might the future manage both high tech and high touch? If the image of the future is a picture of crisis and despair, what trends, left on their current course, would deliver this future? Would our current responses to dangers and threats take even more extreme forms? Questions like these become intriguing hypotheses to use as a guide for learning through environmental scanning.

Exploring Forecasts and Implications for Key Drivers

A good way to experience systems thinking is to explore forecasts and implications for key drivers. One development or choice can put an entire cascade of related actions in motion. Take energy as an example. Right now the race is on for alternatives to fossil fuels, because some forecasting models show that demand will far exceed supply within a decade. Which energy source is likely to be the dominant alternative and what infrastructure would it require? What are the implications for the economy as the winners and losers are sorted out? The forecast could be about lowering demand rather than producing more energy. What large-scale changes in industries, transportation, and home usage could support this alternative?

Or try a more personal type of learning and heat up a health education course with forecasts about the rising incidence of disease from unhealthy behaviors. This is the future speaking to the present while choices can still be made. The implications to individuals and society from such diseases as cancer, diabetes, and dementia are alarming. To make this real, use personal risk factors to play out the likelihood of having a disease and then explore the personal implications for all aspects of life. When modeling and simulations become more sophisticated, this kind of glimpse of a person's possible future could become the ultimate scared-straight experience.

Scanning Beyond the Textbook Version

Older students like a good excuse to show up their elders. Turn that thrill into learning that goes beyond the textbook or other official course material. Whatever the copyright date on the book, it could never be the final word on any subject. To supplement the textbook, urge students to turn to more immediate sources of knowledge like the Web, newspapers, and magazines. Invite experts from the community to talk about some of the more surprising ways a subject is changing. Have students search for forecasts that anticipate what may happen next. Fill the room with photos and headlines that suggest what lies just beyond the textbook version.

Call this exercise "learning for the next edition" and challenge the students to find ideas and developments that really challenge their textbook authors, teachers, and parents. People say they value "out of the box" thinking, but too few people know how to do it. This exercise presumes that thinking out of the box has to be preceded by thinking outside the official textbook.

Exercising the Imagination Through Scenarios

The future is not predetermined. This is easy to say and much harder to comprehend. This can be illustrated in the past through alternative histories or in the future through scenarios. Alternative histories invite us to imagine what would have happened if some key event or condition had been different. What if colonialism had never happened in Africa? How different would the United States be if it had split apart rather than fight the Civil War? We cannot know what the consequences might have been, but we can imagine many stories about how different things would be today.

Likewise, we can take a number of premises about the future and imagine alternative scenarios for how they will play out. A good set of scenarios for a government class might explore levels of engagement in democracy. What is the conventional expectation about civic engagement and the kind of future America it will create? What is the dark-side expectation about declining involvement and polarization, and what are the consequences? Would a scenario for an aspirational future involve a viable multiparty system or online voting on civic referenda? Would a visionary future engage people of all generations in profound discussions about opportunity, equity, and well-being?

Scenarios are experiential learning about the future, and the more memorable the experience, the more meaningful the learning. While scenarios are typically written stories, they could be artistic images, one-act plays, or videos. In fact, these art forms may help capture the emotional dimension of alternative futures in a more compelling way than words.

FORESIGHT PRACTICES FOR LEADERS

Taking Inventory of Learning Needs

Schools are preparing students to succeed in the future. If school leaders are not constantly asking what their students will need to know in that future, they are failing them. Does the core curriculum teach students to learn and adapt in a changing world? Is the emphasis right within the curriculum?

If creativity and innovation are the new value creators in the economy, where is this learning occurring and is it sufficient to the task? If lifelong learning is a given, where in the curriculum are the skills of self-directed learning taught? Assessing the future is the only way to arrive at learning outcomes that can stand the tests of time and change.

Education leaders who don't have at least a rudimentary system for scanning the future might as well be flying blind into the unknown. Since leaders by definition have followers, this is irresponsible. This denial of the future can even be immoral.

Understanding Push, Pull, and Weight

Leaders need to pay great attention to external forces of change that are "pushed" on us, like new technologies, political decisions, or the ups and downs of the economy. They cannot afford to be blindsided by trends, issues, and events. They also play an important role in interpreting implications for their organizations.

Leaders who recognize the power of pull from internal forces can lead people to shape their future. Setting direction is the critical learning task for leaders. The more effective we are in working with vision, goals, and strategies, the more we can contribute to shaping the future. The future cannot be controlled, but it can be influenced through the power that comes from pull.

Weight requires a different kind of awareness. As the serenity prayer goes, "Grant me the wisdom to accept the things I cannot change, courage to change the things I can, and the wisdom to know the difference." An awareness of weight does not force leaders to give into the status quo. Leaders simply learn to appreciate what may be involved in any change and the time that may be needed to change attitudes and structures.

Wise leaders also recognize and preserve the weight of matters that should not change. School administrators and teachers regularly stand up for weight of the right kind. Many try to keep schools from growing too large for students to be known, or work to counter the tendency to put standardized curriculum ahead of individual creativity and initiative.

Outsmarting the Forecasts

Many people expect that accurate forecasts are the most valuable. In reality, as Yale Uiniversity sociology professor emitus points out, the most valuable forecasts are the ones leaders choose to negate:

> For example, the prediction that in five years the schools will be unable to accommodate all the students, if based on reliable and valid population projections, is presumptively true at the time it is made. . . . Because the city council does decide to build more schools, the original prediction turns out to be self-denying and terminally false. Thus, it is much too simple to evaluate a prediction by whether or not the prediction turns out to be true or false in the end. Predictions can be useful precisely because they lead to action that negates them. (Bell, 2002, p. 40)

A leader should always be thinking about which forecasts need to be negated. If student achievement data is trending down, how can a forecast predicting that large numbers of students will fail a standards test required for high school completion be averted? If teacher shortages are projected, how can recruitment efforts change this outcome? Leaders have to be aware of the future they need to try to avert.

Rejecting the Official Future as Reality

The "official future" takes for granted that current conditions will continue, perhaps with some incremental improvement. For leaders this can become the complacent future, which might be the future that will not challenge schools to do the most they can for students and the community. The hardest task may be speaking this truth to power in a contented community.

Leaders need ways to uncover these assumptions. One place to see the official future is in public relations rhetoric, where the public is told what it wants to hear. Another way to find the "official future" is to ask people in community-wide discussions. The question is straightforward: Given our current course, what do you think our schools will be like in 10 years?

Provocative forecasts and scenarios can be used to shake up this complacent thinking. An undesirable but plausible forecast or scenario can prompt people to think seriously about what they do not want to happen in their community. If they see the official future as insufficient to avoid their fears or achieve their highest hopes, they are more likely to abandon a comfortable course.

THE FUTURE OF FORESIGHT IN LEARNING

To use foresight effectively in learning, we need more research on how children's views of the future vary by gender, social class, and ethnic group (Hicks, 2003, p. 61). How do images of the future affect learning and shape behavior? Foresight research tends to focus more on how individuals and organizations make decisions rather than on how well foresight aids their learning. Even less is known about teaching foresight to school-age children, and in this era of evidence-based practices, the propositions in this book will need to be subjected to this rigor.

The biggest open question about foresight is what it will take to give prospective learning as much standing within the curriculum as retrospective learning. There is a long history of teaching and testing established knowledge. There are no future facts. What is the evidence that someone has acquired foresight knowledge and skills? How can we test the capacity to think about the future when the real test doesn't come until later, when we can see the results of our collective decisions in creating the future?

e ⌐

RECOMMENDED RESOURCES

A Starter Set of Trends to Explore

The Institute for Alternative Futures, a nonprofit organization that leads in the discovery and creation of preferred futures, compiled this list for its workshops to give people a jump-start in brainstorming trends. These trends, issues, and developments come from various environmental scans IAF conducted in the last 10 years. For more information on scans, forecasts and scenarios, visit www.altfutures.com.

1. *Who are we becoming?*

Population growth	Aging populations
Cultural diversity	Ethnic shift
Inclusivity	Rise of creative class
Generational synergy	Performance enhancements

2. *What will our world be like?*

Globalization	Security
Biological globalization	Species migration
Global warming	Water shortages
Urban living	Sprawl
Healthy buildings	Historic preservation

3. *How will we learn?*

Distributed learning	Individualized learning
Learning culture	Lifelong learning
Communities of practice	Innovation
Learning organizations	Just-in-time

4. *What capabilities will we have?*

Surveillance society	Smarter markets
Mass customization	Web technology
Mobile communications	Personal publishing—blogs
Hydrogen economy	Micropower
Nanotechnology	Genomics

5. *What will organizations become?*

Self-organizing	Networks
Swarm activism	Decline in civic engagement

Corporate fraud	Corporate social responsibility
Talent wars	Transparency

6. *What values will guide us?*

Meaning matters	Trust
Spirituality	Access
Fairness	Human rights
Quality of life	Democracy

Lessons From Using Scenarios

This summary of what is gained through scenarios comes from Robert Olson (personal communication), senior fellow with the Institute for Alternative Futures, and is based on IAF's 28 years of experience in scenario development.

Expand Your Field of View: People tend to see what they expect to see. Things that don't fit into our expectations and assumptions often don't get noticed. Looking at events through explicit and significantly different images of how events may unfold allows us to see more of what's happening.

Achieve a Strategic Perspective: We tend to be preoccupied with the details of daily news, short-term business tactics, and organizational operations. Scenarios allow us to think about what is really going on behind the big story and the different ways that events could unfold in the future.

Create a Basis for Ongoing Learning and Strategic Conversation: People deeply involved in scenario thinking become highly motivated to have ongoing strategic conversations about "what's happening" and "where things are going." All participants become more aware of their underlying assumptions and the range of key forces driving change.

Create a Framework for Ongoing Environmental Scanning: Environmental scanning efforts that use scenarios as a lens for looking at ongoing developments will "pick up" more and more relevant information. "Signposts" or "early indicators" of one or another scenario can be used as a framework for scanning.

Clarify and Elevate Aspirations: Some scenarios within a scenario set should represent both conventional and visionary views of the "preferred future." Using these scenarios helps clarify a direction around high aspirations.

Generate Strategic Initiatives: Understanding key forces driving change, thinking strategically about different ways the future might unfold, and clarifying aspirations are ideal preparation for developing strategic initiatives.

Evaluate Initiatives to Identify "Robust" Options: New and existing strategies can be evaluated by testing them against a set of scenarios and asking: Are they robust enough to work in most or all scenarios or would they only produce the intended results in limited, special circumstances?

Keep "on Track" for Goals: Scenarios can help us think through the changes that may be necessary to keep on track for our goals, even if the circumstances we encounter in the future are very different from those we imagine today.

Enhance Participation in Strategic Planning: Conversations and planning exercises developed around vivid scenarios grab people's interest and make it easier to involve more people in strategic planning efforts.

Build Support for New Initiatives: Involving people in scenario thinking, generating strategic initiatives, and evaluating initiatives to identify robust options build support for the ideas that emerge from and survive this process.

Sources of Information to Use in Foresight

New Horizons for Learning has served as a resource and clearinghouse for educational change since 1980. Its website features information and articles on the future, neuroscience, lifelong learning, teaching, and learning strategies and special needs. Dee Dickinson is the educator and visionary who founded this widely respected and forward-thinking organization. The website is www.newhorizons.org.

The World Future Society (WFS) and Global Schoolnet (GSN) have agreed to collaborate in creating foresight-related materials and learning activities, including a new education competition to challenge students to think about the future. GSN uses a variety of project-based approaches focusing on collaboration and community building and includes subject matter from diplomacy and geography to history and journalism.

These magazines and journals feature information on trends, forecasts, scenarios, and other foresight methodologies:

- *The Futurist*, a publication of the World Future Society
- *Future Survey*, a publication of the World Future Society
- *Futures Research Quarterly*
- *Foresight: Journal of Futures Studies*

These websites offer reports and other examples of learning from foresight:

- www.altfutures.com, Institute for Alternative Futures
- www.wfs.org, World Future Society
- www.gbn.org, Global Business Network
- www.iftf.org, Institute for the Future
- www.shell.com/scenarios, Shell Oil scenarios

4

THE INTEGRAL ROLE
OF IDENTITY IN
SHAPING THE FUTURE

Our interior state may be of greater consequence to the future than anything that happens out there in the exterior world. Our identity determines how we act in the present and what becomes important for us to create in the future. In anticipatory learning, we study how our identity shapes our evolution as individuals, organizations, and societies. What we learn and do is bounded by our values, beliefs, ethics, emotions, and intelligence. If our identity becomes bound in a way that is no longer useful, anticipatory learning enables us to adapt how we think about ourselves and our world.

Learning is not about acquiring more information; rather, as organizational learning expert Peter Senge (1990) says, it is about "expanding the ability to produce the results we truly want in life" (p. 142). We need a "relentless willingness to root out the ways we limit or deceive ourselves from seeing what is, and to continually challenge our theories of why things are the way they are" (p. 159). These mental models are "deeply held internal images of how the world works" which can "limit us to familiar ways of thinking and acting" (p. 174).

A SENSITIVE ROLE FOR SCHOOLS

After families, schools may well have the most influence on identity. When young people succeed, we credit their schools for developing their capabilities.

Schools are at their worst when they fail to give students confidence in themselves and their potential for the future.

Schools shape our collective identity by teaching us about our culture. According to futurist and educator Peter Bishop (2002), "Culture includes a people's beliefs about itself and the world, values, norms of conduct, customs and manners. Culture is tradition, the repository of that people's experience: what works, what to avoid, how to survive and prosper in the world" (p. 136).

This is a delicate tension for schools to negotiate: we expect schools to transmit our collective identity, develop our individual potential, and prepare us to adapt to succeed in the future. To negotiate this tension with integrity and transparency, schools can do a better job of helping students understand how their identity is constructed and why that matters to the future.

> The human idea of the future is not only based on a sharp analysis of a single moment or action and its varying factors, it is also affected by emotions, fears, hopes, personal history, and experiences, as well as the general views, values and opinions shared by society and the environment. The orientation toward the future is based on how these images become parts of a person's reality and thus also how they become determinants of his or her behavior and decision making. (Rubin, 2002, p. 301)

To help students understand their personal experiences and motivations, schools can introduce knowledge from psychology, religion, philosophy, and spirituality. To teach about culture and society, schools can draw from sociology and anthropology. Anticipatory learning integrates these learning disciplines and their practices to understand the interplay between our beliefs about ourselves and what we choose for our future.

A CHANGING CONTEXT FOR IDENTITY

Our identities must have seemed more certain in periods of less mobility and technological change. A child growing up in an isolated and primitive village would have experienced the developmental stages of life—child, adult, and elder—and her different roles—daughter, mother, friend—in relationship to others in the village. Otherwise, the influences of culture and capabilities available to shape her identity would seem very limited.

In today's global bazaar of cultures and capabilities, a child has a lot more to assimilate into her identity. Identity is not up for grabs in this changing world. If it were, human nature would change much more rapidly than it does. However, the quantity and volatility of influences is great enough to make cultivating a clear sense of personal identity a priority for everyone.

Today, finding a remote village untouched by globalization would be hard to do. Food, natural resources, and manufactured goods move around the planet, pulling local economies into close commerce. Western science, technology, and entertainment are still significant cultural forces, but education and economic opportunity are spreading across a global economy, bringing other cultures into play. We are all becoming citizens of the world.

There are few enclaves of sameness anywhere today. Schools in many small towns are just as likely as urban schools to experience substantial demographic change. Old census categories for defining race or ethnicity are becoming archaic as America becomes a nation where the majority is made up of minorities. Many urban schools are centers of multiculturalism. Schools are even faced with altered social expectations about sexuality and gender roles.

Individuals with mental illness experience another form of identity crisis. Many children now experience the imposed stress of an accelerated life as the "hurried child." The National Institute of Mental Health (2005) estimates about 1 in 10 children suffer from mental illness severe enough to cause some level of impairment. Because many serious mental disorders tend to strike in childhood, adolescence, and young adulthood, schools are frontline responders to these problems.

In the future, what it means to be human could well be in question. Drugs and machines will be available to enhance intelligence and physical ability. The World Transhumanist Association (2005) declares that "we foresee the feasibility of redesigning the human condition, including such parameters as the inevitability of aging, limitations on human and artificial intellects, unchosen psychology, suffering, and our confinement to the planet earth." The debates of yesteryear about whether to allow students to use calculators on math tests will seem quaint when native intelligence can be enhanced by neural implants and ambient computing.

OUR EVOLVING SENSE OF SELF

As the accepted story of human development goes, our human instincts and base needs control us until we are socialized into the culture. We then differentiate from conformity with the culture as we self-actualize. Many religions and spiritual disciplines say our final stage of evolution is a spiritual oneness with others. Picture a developmental line that zigzags from individual to collective at ever-higher stages of development. What this story of human development can obscure with its upward movement is how we are always able to function at a lower developmental level if needed.

Noted psychology professor and author Mihaly Csikszentmihalyi (1993) says the self is constantly being defined and redefined: "We usually think of [self] as a force, a spark, an inner flame with an indivisible integrity. Yet from what we know now, the self is more in the nature of a figment of the imagination, something we create to account for the multiplicity of impressions, emotions, thoughts, and feelings that the brain records in consciousness" (p. 216).

Psychologist Kenneth Gergen (1991) explains self as evolving in relation to others. "We come to be aware that each truth about ourselves is a construction of the moment, true only for a given time and within certain relationships" (p. 16). Since we don't live in that hypothetical remote village, our number of potential relationships is growing exponentially. We acquire new patterns of thinking, behaviors, and values from these relationships. We also acquire an awareness of alternative identities through television, movies, and other forms of mass communication. Gergen says, "in the postmodern world there is no individual essence to which one remains true or committed. One's identity is continuously emergent, re-formed, and redirected as one moves through the sea of ever-changing relationships. In the case of 'Who am I?' it is a teeming world of provisional possibilities" (p. 139).

With so much complexity to absorb into identity, is it any surprise that schools are much more confident in educating people about their exterior world than helping them understand their interior world? Yet without understanding identity, anticipatory learning is not possible. We cannot understand future possibilities or collaborate in creating preferred futures until we grasp how much of what we see today and expect tomorrow comes from inside us. Fortunately there are methodologies and practices that open windows into identity. While these windows do not make everything clear, they do make what is happening more apparent to us.

WINDOWS INTO COLLECTIVE IDENTITY

Using Metaphors as Clues

Whenever we get stumped about how to explain something conceptual or complex, we turn to metaphors. All communication is laced with symbolism. Introducing metaphor as an example of a "window" into identity proves just how reliant we are on symbolic language. We not only talk in metaphors, but some cognitive scientists believe we think and reason in them.

> Because [metaphors] embody that "something vague, unknown or hidden," they give concrete form to the inexpressible. Because they make use of every-day concrete things to illustrate the intangible, complex and relational aspects of life, they are vivid and memorable. And because of isomorphism, only the essence of an experience needs to be captured; the rest can be reconstructed from inferential knowledge. In short, metaphors carry around a great deal of information in a compact and memorable package. (Lawley & Tompkins, 2002, p. 9)

These patterns of language reveal how we make sense of the world. A prevalent example of an extended metaphor of modern times is using machine imagery to explain people, organizations, and natural phenomenon. A machine metaphor reveals nicely how much we value control, efficiency, and productivity. Another powerful metaphor of our times is the ecosystem as we strive to understand interconnectedness, adaptation, and self-organizing systems. People use this imagery to describe the World Wide Web, which itself has become a metaphor for explaining how people and organizations interact in a networked world. People describe sequencing of the human genome as the "book of life," and then opt for calling it the "alphabet" in recognition of how more we have to learn. Just nine words and two metaphors sum up one of the greatest identity changes in the teaching profession: sage on the stage or guide on the side.

Our everyday conversations are laden with the meaning we make of our world. Identifying metaphors and discussing what they reveal helps us think critically about our sense making. Are our metaphors revealing some things and obscuring others? If we are indeed thinking and reasoning in metaphors, then it is dangerous not to question the ones we use. If we are trying to create something new, then we need to think carefully about the metaphors we choose to describe it. If people have never imagined this new thing, they will build their understanding on the foundation of what we say it is most like in the present.

Stating Intent Through Values

While values can be simply defined as worthwhile qualities or principles, getting people to define the qualities of any single value is anything but simple. Take honor as an example. Honor is such an important value in education that we have honor codes, honor rolls, and honors programs. When honor is embodied in a code, the intent is to encourage personal integrity and character. When it is an adjective before rolls, it means glory or recognition. When it defines programs, the most accurate definition would come closer to achievement.

Values work in dynamic tension with one another. When we endorse one value, it often affects how much priority we can place on another important value. For example, a school that declares merit to be an important value may find this statement of intention affects its commitment to the important value of equality.

Core values define an organization's essential character. They set expectations and inspire us to align our actions and behaviors with this character. The most credible values reflect the highest intent of everyone within the organization. Core values express how we want to relate to each other and to our purpose.

While values clarify our priorities, there can be a large gap between what we espouse as our intent and what we actually enact as our values. Our world is rife with examples of espoused values and behaviors that enact competing values. We may say we value wholeness and then set course requirements that are long on English, math, and science and short on recreation, creativity, and reflection. A government may say it values fiscal responsibility, but the actions of its leaders reveal a higher priority for popularity and power. A community may say it is warm and welcoming while it refuses to make adequate services available to those who need them.

Values can be used as a reality check. When students define a value and describe its use, they gain more understanding of its various meanings. When people identify values they think are most important, we can ask them to consider whether these values are reflected in the world they are creating. Very different pictures often emerge when different members of an organization list the values that define the organization's character. School administrators and school custodians may have different perspectives on values like fairness, integrity, and respect. People can say which values should define their future and then check these against the values that are defining present conditions. Changing our values will help us choose behaviors and priorities that are much more likely to create the conditions we say we want.

Mining the Depths of Sense Making

Causal layered analysis is a methodology for gaining deeper understanding about the causes of present or future conditions. As futurist Sohail Inayatullah (2003) defines the levels of causal layered analysis, the surface level is the litany or the official public description of the issue. For example, popular news magazines may note that teen pregnancy is decreasing. When we look at the systemic level for the cause of this trend, we may probe the social, political, economic, or cultural strategies that led to decreased teen pregnancy. These might include public health education, availability of birth control, social welfare programs, or cultural norms about children out of wedlock. If we go even deeper and examine this trend at the worldview level, we may find that higher expectations for young women in society could be a significant cause. At the level of our myths, which is the deepest level of understanding, we may find young women reconnecting to ancient stories of the good mother and defining motherhood in terms of responsibility to the next generation.

No view is the correct and complete view of the reality that teenage pregnancy has declined. Casual layered analysis shows how the future can be constructed at various levels. If a decrease in teenage pregnancies stalls, public health leaders could find an alternative strategy at another level of analysis that will lead to further declines. "Causal layered analysis transforms the litany of a particular future by nesting it in systems, worldviews and myths. The deconstructed future thus can be reconstructed by switching to an alternative system, worldview or myth" (Inayatullah, 2003, p. 37).

Encountering Alternative Cultures

An effective way to help people see their cultures as less absolute is to study other cultures. The way of life we take for granted is just one of many options. Comparing and contrasting cultures helps us see our own culture more clearly. Cross-cultural experiences help us step into the logic and emotions of people with different worldviews. We learn to respect their aspirations. We may even encompass their understanding of the world into our own definition of self.

Schools have always played a role in cross-cultural learning by introducing students to the history, geography, and culture of different countries. In anticipatory learning, schools take the additional step of using this learning to expand our understanding of ourselves. The security and sustainability of the Earth depends on how well we can relate to others within a larger identity of world citizen.

Windows Into Individual Identity

Schools are quite quick to assess their students' cognitive ability, but they are less eager to help students assess their individual aptitudes and preferences. Most school psychologists, social workers, and counselors are expected to use their knowledge and skills to intervene in learning and behavioral problems. In public schools they are rarely directed to help all students achieve their potential. Schools should give all students windows through which to view their strengths and capabilities. These windows into individual identity are multiple intelligences, learning style preferences, personality preferences, and emotional intelligence.

When customized learning becomes a reality, students could have a personal development plan that aligns education opportunities with both their academic interests and what they may need to develop their personal potential. Some of this happens now, when parents intuitively urge their academically gifted children to study music or art or join school clubs. This process could be more intentional with schools and students collaborating to create self-awareness and personal fulfillment along with academic achievement.

Cultivating Multiple Dimensions of Intelligence

Anticipatory learning integrates many ways of knowing and interacting with our world. Educators owe much to Dr. Howard Gardner for his work in defining intelligence as having eight dimensions: linguistic, logical-mathematical, visual-spatial, bodily-kinesthetic, musical, interpersonal, intra-personal, and naturalist. Unfortunately, schools, other institutions, and even societies come to value one or more intelligences greater than the others. This diminishes our integrity as individuals and our ability to create whole-ness in the world.

As Table 4.1 on the dimensions of anticipatory learning indicates, collec-tively the discipline makes use of every type of intelligence. Certain dimensions

Table 4.1 Dimensions of Anticipatory Learning

Multiple Intelligences	Foresight	Identity	Direction Setting	Innovation
Linguistic (Reading, writing, speaking)	Dominant	Supporting	Supporting	Supporting
Logical-mathematical (Problem-solving, computing, and pattern recognition)	Dominant		Supporting	Dominant
Visual-spatial (Perceiving and creating mental images)		Supporting		Supporting
Bodily-kinesthetic (Physical coordination and dexterity)		Supporting		Supporting
Musical (Music and rhythmic movement)				Supporting
Interpersonal (Interacting with others)		Supporting	Dominant	
Intrapersonal (Self-awareness)		Dominant	Supporting	
Naturalistic (Environmental awareness)	Supporting		Supporting	Supporting

may rely on specific intelligences. For example, the identity dimension requires greater cultivation of our intrapersonal intelligence. The foresight dimension relies on linguistic and logical-mathematical intelligences. The direction-setting dimension relies on capabilities in interpersonal intelligence. The innovation dimension draws on many forms of intelligence, but creativity is enhanced through spatial, bodily-kinesthetic, musical, and naturalist intelligences.

Intrapersonal intelligence involves understanding one's inner world of emotions and thoughts and working more consciously with them. Contemplative practices like meditation and prayer bring individuals in touch with this inner world. In a school setting, Dee Dickinson (2002) recommends exercising intrapersonal intelligence through participating in independent projects, reading illuminating books, journal writing, imaginative activities and games, and finding quiet places for reflection.

Maximizing Different Preferences for Learning

We each have a preferred learning style. A person with strong intrapersonal and interpersonal intelligence knows how to adjust learning styles to become more effective in working with others in anticipatory learning. Some people like words and others like pictures and graphs. Some people want to reflect, some want to talk with others, and still others prefer experience.

Many models have been developed to describe these preferences. Some parallel the multiple intelligences. Others take their cue from sensory preferences (seeing, hearing, listening, doing). Other systems model learning through social interaction. The purpose here is not to endorse any one learning style inventory; rather, it is to point out that being aware of our preferences becomes even more critical in anticipatory learning.

If we prefer concrete experience as a way to learn, we need more diverse experiences to get an accurate perception of how we relate to our world. If we like searching for the meaning of things, we may be particularly adept at reflective observation. If we prefer logic and ideas to feelings, we may interpret our world through theories and ideas. If our preference is learning by doing, we prefer experimenting to find out what really works.

Clarifying Personality Preferences

We also can get a better sense of our own identity by understanding the strengths and weaknesses of our personality. Katherine Briggs and Isabel Myers (as cited in Hirsch & Kummerow, 1987) created an indicator of personality by looking at eight different personal preferences. The widely used and researched Myers Briggs Type Indicator organizes these eight preferences into four bipolar scales to arrive at an individual's preferences on four aspects of personality:

- Extraversion or introversion to describe what people find energizing—the outside world of people, activities, or things or the internal world of ideas, emotions, or impressions.
- Sensing or intuition to describe whether people prefer to take information through the five senses or through a "sixth sense" of what might be.
- Thinking or feeling to describe preferences for deciding, which are either logical and objective or personal and subjective.
- Judgment or perception to describe preferences for living in a planned and organized way or a spontaneous and flexible way.

Two personality preference groupings are more grounded in the present; two are more oriented to the future. People who indicate a preference for sensing and thinking are likely to interpret the present world through facts and cause and effect. They are better managers of the here and now. People who prefer sensing and feeling also define the present world in facts, but they also care about how people are affected. They are great troubleshooters in meeting the daily concerns of people. People who combine preferences for intuition and thinking see the possibilities for the future and can present them through theoretical concepts. They are good designers of the future with an ability to use foresight in direction setting. People with a preference for intuition and feeling see the possibilities and relate well to people's aspirations for achieving an outcome. They connect this strong sense of vision into effective direction setting.

Developing Emotional Intelligence

Cognitive intelligence is not a complete predictor of individual performance in school and work. People can be smart but emotionally and socially inept.

To better understand personal capacity, emotional ability must be combined with cognitive ability. Various psychological inventories have been developed to understand these competencies, according to experts Robert J. Emmerling and Daniel Goleman (2003). "All theories within the emotional intelligence paradigm seek to understand how individuals perceive, understand, utilize and manage emotions in an effort to predict and foster personal effectiveness" (p. 12). Some of the attributes of emotional intelligence are self-awareness, self-regulation, motivation, empathy, interpersonal functioning, stress management, mood, and stress management. Goleman developed a theory of work competence related to leadership that is based on four major domains: self-awareness, self-management, social awareness, and relationship management (Emmerling & Goleman, 2003, p. 16).

IDENTITY PRACTICES FOR LEARNERS

Reflecting on Reality

Anticipatory learning does not cede the possibility of discerning what may be true and reliable about the present or the future. Csikszentmihalyi (1993) recommends we not abandon our attempts to understand reality even though our own sense of reality may not be completely reliable: "The first step to wisdom is to realize that we cannot trust implicitly our senses and beliefs, yet to still be eager to understand the reality that lies behind our partial perceptions of it" (p. 171). If we are humble enough to accept that other interpretations may be as valid as our own, we will question our understanding. If we can observe what is happening with the kind of emotional detachment that yogis advise, we can become more open to all that is occurring.

Organizational learning expert Peter Senge (1990) explains how we shape our view of reality: "Structures of which we are unaware hold us prisoner. Once we can see them and name them, they no longer have the same hold on us. . . . We will probably never perceive fully the multiple ways in which we influence our reality. But simply being open to the possibility is enough to free our thinking" (pp. 160, 170). We have to discipline ourselves to seeing interrelationships, including the role we play in creating the structures that have us trapped. Reflection slows down our thinking processes and helps us see how our mental models are shaping our behaviors and actions.

Typical educational environments are not particularly supportive of reflective learning, which requires freedom from noise and busyness. Reflective learning requires open, unprogrammed time and accepting answers that may not conform to our expectations or results that may not be measurable. Self-reflection is critical in questioning the assumptions we make as individuals and groups.

Listening Together

William Isaacs in *Dialogue and the Art of Thinking Together* (1999) urges us to listen together so that we "take into account not only what things look like from one's own perspective, but how they look and feel from the perspective of the whole web of relationships among the people concerned" (p. 103). To become better listeners, we have to learn to calm our mind and be present. We need to avoid jumping to our own conclusions or reacting out of our own emotional memory. Isaacs says we should look for evidence that challenges or disconfirms our point of view and be conscious of "the ways in which we project our opinions about others onto them, how we color or distort what is said without realizing it."

Collaborative learning works well because it does satisfy this need to listen together. Our understanding expands as we listen to how others understand the issue or situation.

Shifting Our Locus of Control

Essential to believing we can create the future we prefer is a strong internal locus of control. If we have an internal locus of control, we believe that our success or failure results from our own actions. With an external locus of control, we believe that fate or some external force is responsible for the condition of our life. We see ourselves as victims of circumstances.

Senge adds that we may believe we do not deserve what we really want. "Most of us hold one of two contradictory beliefs that limit our ability to create what we really want. The more common belief is our powerlessness—our inability to bring into being all the things we really care about. The other belief centers on unworthiness—that we do not deserve to have what we truly desire" (Senge, 1990, p. 156).

Seeking Wholeness Through Religion and Spirituality

Achieving wholeness can be hard in a secular society with a strict adherence to separation of church and state. Because we are not sure how to integrate religion and spirituality into secular classrooms and workplaces, we fail to acknowledge how this part of our identity also influences how we understand the world.

All the great religious and spiritual disciplines speak to a human desire for wholeness. The great religious and spiritual traditions offer learning practices for identity that have been passed through generations and refined by their experience. They foster principles and practices that push us to be better than we might be if left to our own devices. We are called to work with purpose and passion for something that is larger than our own lives. Our reason is trained through the study of texts that explain the world. Our intuition is heightened through other ways of knowing, such as discernment, meditation, and prayer. We become more compassionate and responsible as we see our connectedness with others. We are inspired to be more committed to serving the common good.

IDENTITY PRACTICES FOR LEADERS

Inclusivity Honors Diverse Identities

Leaders who practice inclusivity have a heightened awareness of different cultures and perspectives and the limits of their own viewpoints. Rather than attempting to assimilate differences, inclusivity sees these differences as "resources for innovating more powerfully, solving problems more effectively, and creating more human and stimulating work environments" (Olson & Dighe, 2001). There are three major tasks in inclusivity:

- Being aware of differences in cultures and perspectives. This includes understanding how our dominant culture inhibits others and how its rules and priorities offer us a flawed view of how the world is.
- Valuing and preserving differences. A process of mutual adaptation and cultural fusion is leading to greater innovation that honors different cultures.

- Synergizing differences into a resource to be used rather than a problem to be solved. Drawing on a rich mix of perceptions and thinking will allow us to become more aware, flexible, and creative.

Using Storytelling to Build Shared Identity

As leaders we can use stories to create shared identity. Telling stories is a bonding ritual, whether the stories are as simple as explaining why we are here or as compelling as what we hope to achieve. To be authentic, stories must embody our own identity and resonate with the identities of our listeners. We have to bring ourselves, including our emotions, into the story to tell a good story. We tell authentic stories to share wisdom and experience, to convey our vision and values, and to inspire people to reach goals.

> A good story is like a mirror that you hold up for others so they see something of themselves reflected back. The central power of any story is that it touches something personal in us. . . . You can rant and rave all you want over people who "won't face the facts" or who "ignore the facts" or who "don't live in the real world," but your facts won't reach them until you give them a new story. . . . If you choose to tell empowering stories you will encounter anger as people defend their "victim stories." When a new story demands courage, extra effort, or invalidates past choices, people usually get defensive. . . . People stick with their story even when presented with facts that don't fit. They simply interpret or discount the facts to fit their story. This is why facts are not terribly useful in influencing others. People don't need new facts—they need a new story. (Simmons, 2002, p. 52–54)

Debunking Limiting Myths

Causal layered analysis takes us to the level of myths to understand how our mental models are defining the world. Gergen (1991) warns against becoming so enchanted with a myth that it operates as a form of cultural blindness. Two myths he cites as worthy of challenge are progress and individualism. He notes that "no advances occur in a social or ecological vacuum" (p. 232) and progress in one domain could actually move other domains backward. Likewise, a strong American belief in individualism blinds us to how much we are influenced by relationships and groups. He counsels that we always consider who benefits and who loses from any particular myth.

What other myths are we accepting that should be challenged? Businesses and communities value growth without recognizing the trade-offs in profitability or sustainability. The American pioneer spirit moving across the country is a myth that favors mobility and works against staying in place and valuing belonging. The myth of the American dream blinds us to seeing that most people do not beat the odds against their success.

Changing Minds Through Multiple Formats

Minds can be changed if we use multiple strategies over a long period of time, according to Gardner (2004). People are more likely to change if their emotions are engaged and they make commitments to new thinking in public. New ways of thinking must be "well stated and well embodied in spoken policy, in modeling behaviors, in groups that actually do what they are empowered to do—then and only then is a major change of mind likely to occur" (p. 15). Gardner (2004) advises using these seven strategies to change minds:

1. Use reason to identify relevant factors and logically assess the new way of thinking.
2. Do research and collect relevant data.
3. Invoke resonance to make the view, idea, or perspective feel right to an individual.
4. Use representational redescriptions in different linguistic, numerical, or graphic ways to reinforce the new thinking.
5. Provide resources and rewards to tip the balance in favor of a new idea.
6. Leverage real-world events to make new thinking possible.
7. Overcome resistances to new thinking.

OPEN QUESTIONS FOR EDUCATORS ABOUT IDENTITY

Futurist Wendy Schultz (interview, August 2, 2004) asks what will happen when an entire generation grows up in layered, multidimensional, multidirectional information environments. Young people will develop new identities as they adapt to chaos and complexity, return to an oral culture thanks to advances in voice recognition, and become hyperlinked, nonlinear thinkers because they use hypermedia in their learning. She asks, "What if all these changes lead to a complete shift in mental structures?"

Gergen (1991) poses a critical question about self in postmodern times. Do we cope with the phenomenon of the saturated self by evolving to a higher level of differentiation and connectedness? Or do we revert to more fixed definitions of identity that are less destabilizing? Educators will find themselves in a tug-of-war between these two evolutionary pathways as people cope with the consequences of a saturated self.

℮ ⌐

RECOMMENDED RESOURCES

Many school districts communicate their identity through statements of core values. Below are three examples that illustrate different personalities, intentions, and priorities.

Ann Arbor Public Schools (2005) is committed to:

- Putting the needs of students first in all decisions and actions
- Having high expectations for all students and staff
- Meeting students' educational and social needs
- Valuing and treating students as individuals
- Serving students, families, and the community in a professional manner
- Facilitating open, inclusive communication within the school and with the greater community
- Encouraging and supporting students to become responsible, independent lifelong learners
- Providing equitable access to opportunities and resources for students
- Practicing mutual respect among students, staff, parents, and community members
- Welcoming parents' involvement in the education of their children
- Maintaining a safe and orderly school environment

Virginia Beach City Public Schools (2005) maintains a commitment to establishing a workforce dedicated to the education of our youth and creating an environment conducive to productivity for the benefit of both staff and students. To support this philosophy, the school division has established a set of values for all employees referred to as The Virginia Beach City Public Schools Core Values.

- Youth (places real value on young people)
  - Has confidence in youth
  - Wants to work around and with young people
  - Obtains satisfaction from seeing young people grow
- Commitment (the dedicated, enthusiastic pursuit of a course of action)
  - Follows through on an obligation in a professional manner
  - Sets high expectations for the accomplishment of personal and professional goals
  - Serves as a positive and loyal ambassador for the school division
- Compassion (an empathetic, understanding, supportive disposition towards others)
  - Speaks with others in a tactful, straightforward, and positive manner
  - Focuses on the process rather than blaming others
  - Expresses an appreciation for others through words and deeds
- Integrity (an honest, ethical, principled approach)
  - Earns the trust of others
  - Does the right thing even if it is difficult or unpopular
  - Acts in the best interest of the school division, not for personal gain
  - Gives an honest report of actions, progress, and results
- Positivity (an optimistic outlook on life)
  - Is hopeful about the future
  - Sees the positive in people and situations
  - Possesses a belief that conditions will improve
- Respect (a willingness to recognize, honor, and value individual contributions and differences)
  - Recognizes others publicly for their contributions
  - Seeks and values feedback from others
  - Shows fair and equitable treatment for others
- Work Ethic (a diligent and consistent approach for producing quality results)
  - Achieves positive results through a continuous improvement process
  - Encourages new and innovative ideas to improve results

- Takes responsibility for one's actions
- Makes a noticeable contribution as a team member
- Wisdom (possessing mature, objective, balanced judgment)
  - Uses knowledge and learnings from past experiences to solve problems
  - Exercises self-control
  - Demonstrates willingness to take intelligent risks

Montgomery County (Maryland) Public Schools (2005) Core Values

Total Child:	We believe that academic, physical, and emotional health; and personal, interpersonal, and career development are fundamental to student success.
Diversity:	We value individual differences and believe that every person is worthy of respect and appreciation.
Equity:	We believe it is the right of every student to have equitable access to educational opportunities.
Collaboration:	We believe that teamwork and partnerships with students, families, MCPS staff, and community stakeholders are essential to achieving success for all students.
Professionalism:	We are committed to integrity, respect, accountability, and professional growth.

5

DIRECTION SETTING FOR PREFERRED FUTURES

Despite the bias of our action-oriented culture to decision making, learning is just as important as deciding in setting direction. Our learning has to go beyond acquiring the technical knowledge and skills to accomplish the required tasks. We need social learning to effectively collaborate in creating preferred futures.

Direction setting forges the learning from foresight and identity into wiser decisions about what to create in the future and how to do it. We define our vision through reflection and strategic conversations, and then we choose goals and actions to achieve our preferred future. Through learning by doing, we continuously test and adapt our action plans to achieve success.

Visions that really live in people can shape the future, according to futurist Clem Bezold (personal communication, September 15, 2004), a leading practitioner of aspirational futures. Authentic visions attract commitment and resources, he says, and align behaviors and actions with the highest contribution people can make to a world that will work for all.

Bold visions are rare. A truly bold vision lifts us right out of our comfort zone of prior knowledge and skills and forces us to learn to do something entirely new and untested with everyone watching. At the outset, what we understand about any vision can be poorly formed. We have to risk failure to be open to surprising success. Anticipatory learning requires an enacted vision. The vision is working on our learning while we are working on our vision.

BOLD DIRECTIONS FOR LEARNING IN A WORLD AT RISK

Groups are quick to blame existing power structures for failures. The correct explanation may be our own limited social skills in working together in groups that self-define our vision, goals, and tasks. The most effective way to increase our capacity to learn and adapt in a changing world is not through transforming institutions or governments. The wiser and more empowering way is to increase our capacity as individuals to take initiative in self-organizing groups. Schools are the logical laboratory for learning together how to face challenges at a scale and complexity we have never seen before.

Our choices create our future. This is why many futurists say a mind change has to precede a preferred future. Minds don't just change. They are changed through new thinking and transformative experiences. Few people are so selfish or so evil that they would choose to live in a hard-times future. Many people simply fail to grasp how their past and present choices are setting a course for a feared future.

We don't have to look any further than our newspapers for evidence of social breakdown in all its forms: polarization, poverty, discrimination, terrorism, war, and even genocide. We live on the verge of irreversible environmental breakdown from climate change, air and water pollution, habitat destruction, and species elimination. Other breakdowns now simmering include global disease, health care crises, energy shortages, economic dislocation, and lack of ethical accountability.

Albert Einstein said, "We can't solve problems by using the same kind of thinking we used when we created them." Likewise, it would be difficult to create a preferred future by using the same kind of learning we used to create our past. If learning outcomes look too much to the past, what becomes important is mastering a body of knowledge. What gets rewarded is individual achievement and expertise, even though the results are reported by schools, school systems, states, or nations. Success is defined as competency in basic skills, achievement of core curriculum, and aptitude for college.

If learning outcomes face forward, knowledge becomes a force field flowing into new possibilities. Students and educators become collaborators in learning that:

- Respects and integrates knowledge and practice across multiple disciplines into greater understanding and performance
- Generates new thinking that leaps over present problems and limitations
- Unifies individual perspectives and strengths into collective intelligence

This is a bold vision for anticipatory learning that will move us into an alternative future for education. The methodologies and practices of direction-setting help us decide as individuals and organizations what our preferred future is and what learning might be required to achieve it.

DIRECTION SETTING METHODOLOGIES IN ANTICIPATORY LEARNING

Appreciating Prior Learning

Let's be clear about orienting learning to the future. We could not dismiss the past and present if we tried. People have to build from what they know to what they don't know. Learning from negative experience and failures may not hold the answer, but such learning effectively eliminates options. Even our most intuitive leaps are informed by past knowledge and insights, even when they happen in an instant and in ways our conscious mind cannot trace. If the past and present are such powerful teachers, beginning with what we have already learned makes sense as the first step in setting new directions.

Appreciative inquiry is a cycle of processes that is similar to the direction-setting process described here. Its particular strength is how well it connects individuals and groups to their own positive energy to create a new future. This energy emerges in the discovery phase, which invites people to celebrate what they have learned and achieved together. Appreciative inquiry begins with dialogue about the defining experiences and successes at the positive core. Beginning with positive dialogue sets a better emotional context than beginning with a problem.

Think of discovery as consolidating our capabilities and confidence that we are up to the next challenge, not because we completed the prerequisite course or managed a passing grade but because we are more aware of what we know and how these lessons prepare us for the next learning challenge.

Where might discovery begin in the classroom? One approach is asking students what they are pleased they have learned in previous classes. By describing what they like best, they reveal both what they assimilated into their own knowledge and how they like to learn. Even asking what students found difficult offers clues about the gaps they still need to address. Discovery through dialogue may never replace pretesting in public school courses, but as an alternative beginning it signals that learning is more than something to be measured. It is something to be experienced.

Discovery is a personal and group reflection that taps into the wisdom Peter Senge and his colleagues (2004) describe in *Presence*: "All learning integrates thinking and doing. In reactive learning, thinking is governed by established mental models and doing is governed by established habits of action. Deeper levels of learning create increasing awareness of the larger whole—both as it is and as it is evolving—that leads to actions that increasingly serve the emerging whole" (p. 8-9).

Framing Learning Through Strategic Conversation

Strategic conversations ground learning in the "what and why" before taking on "how" to do it. In a strategic conversation, we challenge our assumptions with provocative information and questions. We compare and contrast the present with what might be possible in the future. As we listen to different ideas and opinions, we improvise on each other's ideas and beliefs in a free-flowing dialogue.

Strategic conversations are facilitated discussions that are more like Socratic dialogues than lectures or presentations. They are organized around provocative questions like these:

- What is the meaning and purpose of multivariate statistics? What might these models reveal? What might they conceal? Thinking to the future, what challenges might benefit from probability science?
- If the American government is for the people and of the people, what people are present in this telling of westward expansion, who is absent, and why? As new opportunities present themselves in the future, who will have access to the opportunities and what can be done to create greater equity?

- If supply and demand is a fundamental principle of economics, what choices are going into supply and what factors could alter demand? What might become valuable in the future that would not fit so neatly into models of abundance and scarcity?

Defining Strategic Issues for Future Focus

The list of issues and priorities that try to crowd into education is endless and impossible to address. Schools have become the default answer for every social challenge. We have this instinctive sense that future generations can rescue us from our failures. By choosing to address only those issues that rise to the level of a strategic issue, we can use the future as the filter to decide what will be important.

Direction setting is a process of discerning where to focus our attention in anticipatory learning. It is about setting priorities and making choices. Foresight shows us the many things that could happen and the key drivers that are likely to shape alternative futures. Strategic issues are the key drivers we choose to do something about. Strategic issues emerge from a three-part test:

1. They affect our purpose or mission as individuals, communities, or organizations. If we do not do something about them, we lose important options for our future. They affect our ability to realize our potential.
2. We have the ability to intervene in the future and secure a preferred outcome. Someone should have a sense of what capacities are needed to get from where we are now to where we need to be. If the challenge is great, we may need far more learning and preparation to create the capacity to intervene.
3. We are called to leadership that is consistent with our responsibility and vision for the future. Vocations were understood to be calls before they were reduced to occupations. A call speaks to our deepest priorities for our life. This is as true for organizations and communities as it is for individuals.

In democratic cultures, groups do not accept any process that is imposed. Choosing strategic issues is a participatory process. Inviting students to have a say in the strategic issues that will define their learning could increase their commitment and give them a greater stake in the outcome of a course. The youngest children can share some idea about what they think will be important for their future, even if their sense of the future is defined in days and months rather than years.

This is not self-directed learning with all its potential for poorly informed choices. It is learning directed at the future and informed by the knowledge and experience of those who have thoughtfully considered what it might require.

At the school and school system levels, educators and parents can join together to decide which strategic issues are priorities. Gathering the community together to think about the future it wants to create can go by many terms, including futures or vision workshops or search conferences. They are all facilitated experiences in anticipatory learning that use the knowledge from foresight, the awareness of identity, and the discernment of direction setting to focus education on a preferred future.

Expressing Personal Legacies

Legacies are the profound answer to the question every young person gets tired of answering: What do you want to be when you grow up? When we describe the legacy we want, we reveal our highest aspirations for the future. Statements of legacy are simple, unrefined statements of vision. There are a number of simple exercises for inviting people to think about what they would be proudest to create:

- Students could be asked to imagine receiving a prestigious award at a future date like a Nobel Prize or a MacArthur genius award and why they received it.
- They could write a letter to a child in the future describing how they helped create something important to that future.
- They could compose an obituary or describe what people will say at their funeral.

Legacy statements invite us do more than compile a list of achievements; like a scenario, they invite us to try on our preferred future and describe the emotional aspects of that experience. They reveal what we hope our role will be. Legacy exercises remind us to pay attention to the emotional side of direction setting.

Not every legacy exercise requires a lifetime of reflection. It could be just reflecting on the sense of achievement and satisfaction of constructing a term paper on a difficult topic. It might be reflecting on the joy and pride at the end of a choral presentation when the audience stands to applaud. Many students are not sufficiently self-actualized to imagine these outcomes unless they are invited to do so when the learning begins.

Visioning for Great Learning and Doing

Visions express what we want to create in the world. They can take many forms. The most literal vision is a description of a preferred future. This type of vision can be a more detailed and objective description of the future, where the ultimate aspirations of the individual or organization are fulfilled. Visions can be brief statements or a story.

A vision can be a statement of identity that describes who we will be as we stand in our future. For groups, this is a statement of shared identity that unifies people. The most powerful statements of identity often evoke archetypes that are foundational to the human experience: educators as wise elders guiding the young, education as adventures and journeys, and schools as the commons in a learning community.

A vision can be a statement of values that individuals or organizations will use in guiding how they will operate together as they respond to their future. Values like academic freedom, respect for individuals and their gifts, equal opportunity, and education for the whole person are examples of phrases that could be priority values now and in the future.

Visions can be pragmatic or idealistic, long term or short term, as long as they have sufficient emotional power to inspire us to achieve more than we thought possible.

> Visions are not lofty sentiments or inspiring phrases, they're practical tools.
> . . . Visions that have power are expressions of deep purposefulness, acted
> upon in the present moment. . . . First steps are often small, and initial visions
> that focus energy effectively often address immediate problems. What matters

is engagement in the service of a larger purpose rather than lofty aspirations that paralyze action. Indeed, it's a dangerous trap to believe that we can pursue only "great visions." (Senge et al., 2004, p. 142–144)

To be a real force in people's hearts, a vision can never be imposed on a group. Shared visions align people around a collective challenge. We need to ask who should be part of a vision to make it legitimate. Shared visions have a renewing power that comes from people communicating about it as they act together to make it happen. Shared vision has a life of its own because it lives in so many people.

Aspirational visions push at the boundaries of change. Challenges that are easy to meet never elicit the best efforts of a group. Visions that command attention always push against the limits of what we assumed to be possible. Because they often articulate a daring adventure with important outcomes, visions give us the sense we can surpass what we thought were our limits.

As we look at possible visions for schools over the next 10 to 20 years, many possibilities emerge. We see schools at the leading edge of knowledge management, communication, and computing technologies. We see institutional boundaries coming down and students unfettered in pursuing advanced knowledge and skills. We see schools renewing interest in civic engagement and teaching students how to organize around the great challenges of our civilization. We see the opportunity for universities to reorganize around a vision of interdisciplinary learning that transcends the limitations of any single discipline in understanding complex systems.

We can envision schools beginning in preschool to teach health and lifestyle habits of wellness and emotional well-being. We can call on our schools to lead society in enacting a vision of equity and opportunity that closes the have-have not gap. We can envision schools as the local commons where students learn how to make wise choices that have global implications in an interconnected world. The Earth Charter, included at the end of this chapter, is a globally conceived statement of environmental and social stewardship that invites everyone to join in this vision.

Setting Audacious Goals to Push Ahead

Audacious goals are statements of the actions that best exemplify what it will take to achieve our vision. An audacious goal should be so clearly stated that it requires no explanation. It has a clear date by which it will be accomplished and explicit ways to measure whether it has been achieved. Audacious goals help us organize our efforts and measure our success. An audacious goal could take years and, despite all our extraordinary effort, we still might fail to meet it.

What makes these goals audacious is how much they stretch us. Audacious goals go beyond what some people assume is possible or reasonable. The great scientist and science fiction writer Arthur C. Clarke once said that there are four stages of reaction to any truly new idea or audacious goal:

- It's crazy!
- It might be possible, but so what?
- I always knew it was a good idea.
- It was my idea.

The classic example of an audacious goal was President John F. Kennedy's goal to put a man on the moon. A list of other historical examples follows at the end of this chapter. For a team of science students, the audacious goal might be to win the state science fair. For a young writer, the audacious goal might be to have a story published in a quality magazine. For a school whose vision is fostering academic excellence, the audacious goal might be to have 95 percent of its advanced placement students scoring a 3 or above on the exams. For a school system with a vision of integrating the community into learning, the audacious goal might be to have every high school student matched with an adult mentor in a lifelong learning project.

Planning a Course of Action

Selecting a strategy to achieve an audacious goal requires smart thinking about an individual or organization's resources and capabilities. People are prone to see scarcity more than abundance. We can succeed with limited resources if we exercise ingenuity and creativity. Strategies focus our actions, and our action plan orders the tasks and tactics with assignments and timelines.

To illustrate this, let's think about the school system that declares a vision of integrating the community into learning. An audacious goal might be pairing every high school student with an adult mentor in a lifelong learning project. This possibility thinking has to overcome problems of coordination and quality. The school system may choose a strategy of creating a volunteer teacher corps. This gives adults two immediate incentives for lifelong learning: they can gain knowledge and skills in teaching, and they can propose potential areas of study they would enjoy. Students and volunteer teachers could negotiate the nature of the project and define the learning process together. The school system's action plan could provide for a training workshop, a communication system for matching students and adults, and a community awards program that honors mentors and students for outstanding projects each year.

DIRECTION SETTING PRACTICES FOR LEARNERS

In direction setting, an enacted vision is working on our learning while we are working on our vision. Statements of vision are a lot more common than achieved visions. Direction setting fosters the social learning we need to work effectively in social contexts. We learn how our behaviors and those of others affect outcomes. This is learning by experience and models that serve as examples.

Effective groups learn social skills to coordinate their efforts and achieve their goals. They maximize the learning of all members and analyze how well everyone is achieving his or her individual goals. They focus on group and individual accountability for performance and high quality work (Johnson & Johnson, 1997, p. 18).

To work effectively in groups, we need to acquire social skills that enable us to:

- Build trust to promote learning
- Clarify roles within the group
- Establish rules and group norms that work
- Escape victim of circumstance beliefs

Building Trust to Promote Learning

Individuals do not enter new groups with the same willingness to trust. Depending on our past experiences and personalities, we may extend goodwill or distrust. An important initial step in creating a climate for group learning is negotiating trust and levels of intimacy. When a new direction requires risk taking, we need to feel safe enough to talk candidly about our feelings and opinions. Otherwise, we may censor important information that could be the difference between success and failure. Other group behaviors that help build trust and promote learning are ensuring that every voice is heard; validating each other's ideas; and giving feedback that judges the fitness of the work, not the worthiness of the individual.

If we are overly focused on the cognitive dimensions of our tasks, we may fail to discuss how the following factors affect our ability to build trust, create knowledge, and generate change:

- Prior experiences that set the expectations of individuals and the group
- Group norms, whether stated or unstated, that determine behavior
- Assigned or presumed roles that provide identity within the group
- Processes that are prescribed or defined by the group
- Goals and objectives external and internal to the group
- Resources that are available to the group
- Intrinsic and extrinsic rewards for individual and group performance

Clarifying Roles Within the Group

We want to know our identity within the group. We are either assigned or assume roles in groups. Where will we fit in and what kind of behavior will be acceptable? Our identity is defined in part by what we want from the group, what we have to offer it, and whether group goals are consistent with our personal goals. We want to know who will have control over what our group can do and what power and influence our roles have.

Each role has a defined set of appropriate behaviors. When we must play unfamiliar roles in new groups, we can struggle and even revert back to the behaviors of more familiar roles. We can expand our range of behaviors if we learn to experiment with different styles in different groups. If we are accustomed to leading, we should switch to observing the subtle cues and patterns that are harder to see while leading the give and take of group dynamics.

Establishing Rules and Group Norms That Work

Rules can be either stated or unstated expressions of what may or may not be done. Rules encompass how we believe we must act and frame what we accept as true about situations. They are the drivers in the emotional, affective side of groups.

Rules and norms do bring order to our learning. Our brains can do little with random data until it is organized into patterns and theories. People accept rules because they remove ambiguity from situations and create a comfort zone. However, rules are destructive when people are more compliant than effective group functioning requires. When we see rules as limitations, they shackle our thinking.

Rules and norms have power because they control what we see and how we act. They set the boundaries of a group's culture. Groups may even assume rules and limitations where none exist, because what we perceive might as well be true if we are not aware enough to question them. New people are often freer to challenge the rules, because they have not fallen under the group's norms. Rules that lock us into only one way of seeing or operating in the world diminish group effectiveness. One rule that often needs challenging is the tyranny of time in group processes. Reflection, learning, and decision making may not happen on cue. We need to be willing to call our own time-outs when schedules are limiting our learning.

Escaping Victim of Circumstances Beliefs

One of the most difficult lessons to learn is how much we construct our own reality. We are not separate from the systems we want to change. It is easy to get trapped into believing we are victims of circumstances and ascribe the limitations and failures we are experiencing to that all-purpose "they." We are too skilled at externalizing problems and coming up with rationalizations and justifications that blind us to seeing our role in creating our problems. For example, a group of students might advocate a new initiative but fail to gain support from the school administration for unexplained reasons. These advocates then assume all their ideas will not be valued because the administration will not listen anyway. The initiative itself might have had flaws or a timing problem that other initiatives might not have, yet the advocates make a leap of abstraction that they are powerless.

If we can't escape these disempowering beliefs about our circumstances, we get caught in a negative feedback loop. What we believe about our circumstances shapes our behaviors, which in turn feed back into worsening our circumstances. We get trapped in an expiring cycle.

> Only when people begin to see from within the forces that shape their reality and see their part in how those forces might evolve does vision become powerful. . . . Until people can start to see their habitual ways of interpreting a situation, they can't really step into a new awareness. . . . When people who are actually creating a system start to see themselves as the source of their problems, they invariably discover a new capacity to create results they truly desire. (Senge et al., 2004, pp. 45, 136)

DIRECTION-SETTING PRACTICES FOR LEADERS

Directing setting for schools is typically the responsibility of school boards, superintendents, and principals. Anticipatory learning takes direction setting out of this exclusive control and engages everyone in deciding what learning should accomplish. In the living organizations that the future requires, leadership is distributed throughout organizations, and direction setting becomes a shared responsibility.

Students can use these methodologies and practices to define their learning just as appropriately as school boards can use them to plan for the school system's future. Teachers can use these methods to engage students in defining outcomes for a class at its outset. Teachers and administrators can set direction when they update and redesign a curriculum that responds to the future.

Leaders are shifting their direction-setting practices from decision making to empowering people to get things done in a world where self-organizing is replacing command and control. This requires awareness, integrity, and skills in:

- Working with the emotion and energy of visions
- Gauging different interests within groups
- Getting out of the way
- Communicating visions until they come true

Working With the Emotion and Energy of Visions

We rarely create bold visions when things are going great in a perfect world. Visions are a response to a desire for something better. Visions speak to the head and heart of the community. Leaders need empathy to acknowledge the emotions that accompany these times of crisis and risk.

> Once they see clearly their heart's intent, their focus becomes like a laser—a powerful, coherent beam, as opposed to an incandescent, incoherent light. An earnest commitment from the heart emerges, vision becomes clearer, broader, and more inclusive of others. Strength of will is replaced by energetic integrity.... When you see what you're here for, the world begins to mirror your purpose in a magical way. It's almost as if you suddenly find yourself on a stage in a play that was written expressly for you. (Senge et al., 2004, pp. 114, 139)

Gauging Different Interests Within Groups

All groups have individual interests running below the surface. If these interests are not fulfilled when we pursue a shared objective, everyone will not be satisfied and any achievement may be unsustainable. Leaders have to be able to gauge these different interests and how they are shifting.

> Group members usually try to achieve both individual and group goals, and the degree to which they can accomplish this through the same activities determines how effective the group will be in attaining its goals. The situation is further complicated by the fact that most groups and individuals have several goals and different members value different goals at different times and even the same member places different values on the same goal at different times. (Johnson & Johnson, 1997, p. 77)

Leaders have to be careful not to generalize from direct observations. Accepting our assumptions about people's interests without asking them what they want is foolhardy. The wiser course is to ask people to state their interests, and constantly reaffirm that these interests have not shifted over time.

Getting Out of the Way

A hero leader can never be as effective in achieving a vision as a leader who brings together a variety of people with a stake in a successful outcome. The leader has to rein in position power that might undermine a group's autonomy. This can happen even when there is no overt exercise of position power. With a designated leader, group members are prone to pursue only those ideas and avenues that receive validation from the leader. Habits of behavior can be so engrained that people conform to what they believe the leader wants or fail to disagree with a leader even when success is at stake.

Leaders need the wisdom to know when to get out of the way. In a group with shared leadership, the validation comes from the group. More ideas are likely to find receptive listeners. Since power is shared, people are more willing to engage in collaborative rather than competitive behaviors.

Communicating Visions Until They Come True

Visions can lose momentum unless leaders continuously communicate them through their words and deeds. The North Central Regional Education Laboratory (NCREL) advises school leaders to think about "how they spend their time, what they talk about, what problems they solve first, and what they get excited about." In every act, leaders communicate their hopes and dreams and reinforce the values they hold and the vision they hope to achieve. All decision making and governance actions have to build toward the vision.

NCREL recommends these practical tips for communicating visions in schools:

- Posting the vision in a visible place, like the front hallway.
- Reviewing the vision every year in a ceremony that invites staff to recommit to it.
- Addressing the school's vision and mission during assemblies, planning meetings, and school governance council meetings.
- Communicating symbolically through mottos, flags, banners, and materials that are sent out from the school, such as letterheads, pencils, and so forth.

THE FUTURE OF DIRECTION SETTING IN EDUCATION

This chapter proposes using direction setting more pervasively than is typical in most schools. Empowering learners to be involved in their own direction setting could even be controversial, since not every student has the same maturity and motivation to succeed. People have found that giving students meaningful choices does work as an alternative to teacher-directed learning. Where to draw the boundaries around the appropriate level of autonomy will vary in different academic disciplines, class years and levels, and in different communities. Self-directed learning has been largely reserved for the upper levels of college and university education. Although other systems have benefited from people self-organizing to increase responsiveness to the future, this is an untested idea in all but the most limited situations in schools.

There have been many large-scale efforts to create shared visions on matters of public interest. As the issues surrounding schools become more polarized and communities more diverse in their interests, how much more difficult will it be to achieve a shared vision? With the stakes as high as the future of our children, direction setting in schools does seem to be a job for the most skilled facilitators.

With demands for accountability as high as they are in public schools, the tolerance for experimentation seems to have narrowed. What processes and tactics can provide sufficient assurances that all will be well in the present as schools pursue audacious goals for the future?

If social learning is integral to enacted visions, can schools construct field practice for students? Could students take on community problems and create visions and initiatives to pursue a preferred future? Volunteerism, inspired by the future, can create the kind of activism that social innovations require. Could the talents and energy of young people accomplish what their elders have lacked the vision and will to do?

RECOMMENDED RESOURCES

Earth Charter Exemplifies Aspirational Vision and Goals

The Earth Charter is an outstanding example of a statement of vision and audacious goals. It is the product of a decade-long, worldwide, cross-cultural conversation about common goals and shared values. Thousands of individuals and hundreds of organizations from all regions of the world, different cultures, and diverse sectors of society participated. The final version was released in March 2000, following an Earth Charter Commission meeting in Paris at the UNESCO headquarters. The Earth Charter International Secretariat is based at the campus of the University for Peace in San José, Costa Rica. The secretariat provides support for the commission and steering committee, coordinates major programs and global undertakings, and works with a global network of 53 Earth Charter national committees and facilitators, as well as partner organizations, including National Councils for Sustainable Development.

Educators around the world are using the charter in schools, institutions of higher education, communities, and professional development organizations. It is a useful resource to incorporate into courses dealing with themes such as ethics, environment, social justice, sustainable development, globalization, and international relations. Primary school teachers find the Earth Charter an inspiring vehicle for engaging young learners to think positively and creatively about their futures.

According to the Earth Charter Organization (2005), "the most important influences shaping the ideas and values in the Earth Charter are contemporary science, international law, the wisdom of the world's great religions and philosophical traditions, the declarations and reports of the seven UN summit conferences held during the 1990s, the global ethics movement, numerous nongovernmental declarations and people's treaties issued over the past thirty years, and best practices for building sustainable communities."

The Earth Charter, reprinted by permission, follows. Many additional educational resources can be found at www.earthcharter.org.

Preamble

We stand at a critical moment in Earth's history, a time when humanity must choose its future. As the world becomes increasingly interdependent and fragile, the future at once holds great peril and great promise. To move forward we must recognize that in the midst of a magnificent diversity of cultures and life forms we are one human family and one Earth community with a common destiny. We must join together to bring forth a sustainable global society founded on respect for nature, universal human rights, economic justice, and a culture of peace. Towards this end, it is imperative that we, the peoples of Earth, declare our responsibility to one another, to the greater community of life, and to future generations.

Earth, Our Home

Humanity is part of a vast evolving universe. Earth, our home, is alive with a unique community of life. The forces of nature make existence a demanding and uncertain adventure, but Earth has provided the conditions essential to life's evolution. The resilience of the community of life and the well-being of humanity depend upon preserving a healthy biosphere with all its ecological systems, a rich variety of plants and animals, fertile soils, pure waters, and clean air. The global environment with its finite resources is a common concern of all peoples. The protection of Earth's vitality, diversity, and beauty is a sacred trust.

The Global Situation

The dominant patterns of production and consumption are causing environmental devastation, the depletion of resources, and a massive extinction of species. Communities are being undermined. The benefits of development are not shared equitably and the gap between rich and poor is widening. Injustice, poverty, ignorance, and violent conflict are widespread and the cause of great suffering. An unprecedented rise in human population has overburdened ecological and social systems. The foundations of global security are threatened. These trends are perilous—but not inevitable.

The Challenges Ahead

The choice is ours: form a global partnership to care for Earth and one another or risk the destruction of ourselves and the diversity of life. Fundamental changes are needed in our values, institutions, and ways of living. We must realize that when basic needs have been met, human development is primarily about being more, not having more. We have the knowledge and technology to provide for all and to reduce our impacts on the environment. The emergence of a global civil society is creating new opportunities to build a democratic and humane world. Our environmental, economic, political, social, and spiritual challenges are interconnected, and together we can forge inclusive solutions.

Universal Responsibility

To realize these aspirations, we must decide to live with a sense of universal responsibility, identifying ourselves with the whole Earth community as well as our local communities. We are at once citizens of different nations and of one world in which the local and global are linked. Everyone shares responsibility for the present and future well-being of the human family and the larger living world. The spirit of human solidarity and kinship with all life is strengthened when we live with reverence for the mystery of being, gratitude for the gift of life, and humility regarding the human place in nature.

We urgently need a shared vision of basic values to provide an ethical foundation for the emerging world community. Therefore, together in hope we affirm the following interdependent principles for a sustainable way of life as a common standard by which the conduct of all individuals, organizations, businesses, governments, and transnational institutions is to be guided and assessed.

Principles

I. Respect and Care for the Community of Life

    1. Respect Earth and life in all its diversity.

        a. Recognize that all beings are interdependent and every form of life has value regardless of its worth to human beings.

        b. Affirm faith in the inherent dignity of all human beings and in the intellectual, artistic, ethical, and spiritual potential of humanity.

    2. Care for the community of life with understanding, compassion, and love.

        a. Accept that with the right to own, manage, and use natural resources comes the duty to prevent environmental harm and to protect the rights of people.

        b. Affirm that with increased freedom, knowledge, and power comes increased responsibility to promote the common good.

    3. Build democratic societies that are just, participatory, sustainable, and peaceful.

        a. Ensure that communities at all levels guarantee human rights and fundamental freedoms and provide everyone an opportunity to realize his or her full potential.

        b. Promote social and economic justice, enabling all to achieve a secure and meaningful livelihood that is ecologically responsible.

    4. Secure Earth's bounty and beauty for present and future generations.

        a. Recognize that the freedom of action of each generation is qualified by the needs of future generations.

        b. Transmit to future generations values, traditions, and institutions that support the long-term flourishing of Earth's human and ecological communities.

In order to fulfill these four broad commitments, it is necessary to:

II. Ecological Integrity

    5. Protect and restore the integrity of Earth's ecological systems, with special concern for biological diversity and the natural processes that sustain life.

a. Adopt at all levels sustainable development plans and regulations that make environmental conservation and rehabilitation integral to all development initiatives.

b. Establish and safeguard viable nature and biosphere reserves, including wild lands and marine areas, to protect Earth's life support systems, maintain biodiversity, and preserve our natural heritage.

c. Promote the recovery of endangered species and ecosystems.

d. Control and eradicate non-native or genetically modified organisms harmful to native species and the environment, and prevent introduction of such harmful organisms.

e. Manage the use of renewable resources such as water, soil, forest products, and marine life in ways that do not exceed rates of regeneration and that protect the health of ecosystems.

f. Manage the extraction and use of non-renewable resources such as minerals and fossil fuels in ways that minimize depletion and cause no serious environmental damage.

6. Prevent harm as the best method of environmental protection and, when knowledge is limited, apply a precautionary approach.

a. Take action to avoid the possibility of serious or irreversible environmental harm even when scientific knowledge is incomplete or inconclusive.

b. Place the burden of proof on those who argue that a proposed activity will not cause significant harm, and make the responsible parties liable for environmental harm.

c. Ensure that decision making addresses the cumulative, long-term, indirect, long distance, and global consequences of human activities.

d. Prevent pollution of any part of the environment and allow no build-up of radioactive, toxic, or other hazardous substances.

e. Avoid military activities damaging to the environment.

7. Adopt patterns of production, consumption, and reproduction that safeguard Earth's regenerative capacities, human rights, and community well-being.

a. Reduce, reuse, and recycle the materials used in production and consumption systems, and ensure that residual waste can be assimilated by ecological systems.

b. Act with restraint and efficiency when using energy, and rely increasingly on renewable energy sources such as solar and wind.

    c. Promote the development, adoption, and equitable transfer of environmentally sound technologies.

    d. Internalize the full environmental and social costs of goods and services in the selling price, and enable consumers to identify products that meet the highest social and environmental standards.

    e. Ensure universal access to health care that fosters reproductive health and responsible reproduction.

    f. Adopt lifestyles that emphasize the quality of life and material sufficiency in a finite world.

8. Advance the study of ecological sustainability and promote the open exchange and wide application of the knowledge acquired.

    a. Support international scientific and technical cooperation on sustainability, with special attention to the needs of developing nations.

    b. Recognize and preserve the traditional knowledge and spiritual wisdom in all cultures that contribute to environmental protection and human well-being.

    c. Ensure that information of vital importance to human health and environmental protection, including genetic information, remains available in the public domain.

III. Social and Economic Justice

9. Eradicate poverty as an ethical, social, and environmental imperative.

    a. Guarantee the right to potable water, clean air, food security, uncontaminated soil, shelter, and safe sanitation, allocating the national and international resources required.

    b. Empower every human being with the education and resources to secure a sustainable livelihood, and provide social security and safety nets for those who are unable to support themselves.

    c. Recognize the ignored, protect the vulnerable, serve those who suffer, and enable them to develop their capacities and to pursue their aspirations.

10. Ensure that economic activities and institutions at all levels promote human development in an equitable and sustainable manner.

    a. Promote the equitable distribution of wealth within nations and among nations.

    b. Enhance the intellectual, financial, technical, and social resources of developing nations, and relieve them of onerous international debt.

    c. Ensure that all trade supports sustainable resource use, environmental protection, and progressive labor standards.

    d. Require multinational corporations and international financial organizations to act transparently in the public good, and hold them accountable for the consequences of their activities.

11. Affirm gender equality and equity as prerequisites to sustainable development and ensure universal access to education, health care, and economic opportunity.

    a. Secure the human rights of women and girls and end all violence against them.

    b. Promote the active participation of women in all aspects of economic, political, civil, social, and cultural life as full and equal partners, decision makers, leaders, and beneficiaries.

    c. Strengthen families and ensure the safety and loving nurture of all family members.

12. Uphold the right of all, without discrimination, to a natural and social environment supportive of human dignity, bodily health, and spiritual well-being, with special attention to the rights of indigenous peoples and minorities.

    a. Eliminate discrimination in all its forms, such as that based on race, color, sex, sexual orientation, religion, language, and national, ethnic or social origin.

    b. Affirm the right of indigenous peoples to their spirituality, knowledge, lands and resources and to their related practice of sustainable livelihoods.

    c. Honor and support the young people of our communities, enabling them to fulfill their essential role in creating sustainable societies.

    d. Protect and restore outstanding places of cultural and spiritual significance.

IV. Democracy, Nonviolence, and Peace

13. Strengthen democratic institutions at all levels, and provide transparency and accountability in governance, inclusive participation in decision making, and access to justice.

    a. Uphold the right of everyone to receive clear and timely information on environmental matters and all development plans and activities which are likely to affect them or in which they have an interest.

b. Support local, regional and global civil society, and promote the meaningful participation of all interested individuals and organizations in decision making.

c. Protect the rights to freedom of opinion, expression, peaceful assembly, association, and dissent.

d. Institute effective and efficient access to administrative and independent judicial procedures, including remedies and redress for environmental harm and the threat of such harm.

e. Eliminate corruption in all public and private institutions.

f. Strengthen local communities, enabling them to care for their environments, and assign environmental responsibilities to the levels of government where they can be carried out most effectively.

14. Integrate into formal education and life-long learning the knowledge, values, and skills needed for a sustainable way of life.

a. Provide all, especially children and youth, with educational opportunities that empower them to contribute actively to sustainable development.

b. Promote the contribution of the arts and humanities as well as the sciences in sustainability education.

c. Enhance the role of the mass media in raising awareness of ecological and social challenges.

d. Recognize the importance of moral and spiritual education for sustainable living.

15. Treat all living beings with respect and consideration.

a. Prevent cruelty to animals kept in human societies and to protect them from suffering.

b. Protect wild animals from methods of hunting, trapping, and fishing that cause extreme, prolonged, or avoidable suffering.

c. Avoid or eliminate to the full extent possible the taking or destruction of non-targeted species.

16. Promote a culture of tolerance, nonviolence, and peace.

a. Encourage and support mutual understanding, solidarity, and cooperation among all peoples and within and among nations.

b. Implement comprehensive strategies to prevent violent conflict and use collaborative problem solving to manage and resolve environmental conflicts and other disputes.

    c. Demilitarize national security systems to the level of a non-provocative defense posture, and convert military resources to peaceful purposes, including ecological restoration.

    d. Eliminate nuclear, biological, and toxic weapons and other weapons of mass destruction.

    e. Ensure that the use of orbital and outer space supports environmental protection and peace.

    f. Recognize that peace is the wholeness created by right relationships with oneself, other persons, other cultures, other life, Earth, and the larger whole of which all are a part.

The Way Forward

As never before in history, common destiny beckons us to seek a new beginning. Such renewal is the promise of these Earth Charter principles. To fulfill this promise, we must commit ourselves to adopt and promote the values and objectives of the charter.

This requires a change of mind and heart. It requires a new sense of global interdependence and universal responsibility. We must imaginatively develop and apply the vision of a sustainable way of life locally, nationally, regionally, and globally. Our cultural diversity is a precious heritage and different cultures will find their own distinctive ways to realize the vision. We must deepen and expand the global dialogue that generated the Earth Charter, for we have much to learn from the ongoing collaborative search for truth and wisdom.

Life often involves tensions between important values. This can mean difficult choices. However, we must find ways to harmonize diversity with unity, the exercise of freedom with the common good, short-term objectives with long-term goals. Every individual, family, organization, and community has a vital role to play. The arts, sciences, religions, educational institutions, media, businesses, nongovernmental organizations, and governments are all called to offer creative leadership. The partnership of government, civil society, and business is essential for effective governance.

In order to build a sustainable global community, the nations of the world must renew their commitment to the United Nations, fulfill their obligations under existing international agreements, and support the implementation of Earth Charter principles with an international legally binding instrument on environment and development.

Let ours be a time remembered for the awakening of a new reverence for life, the firm resolve to achieve sustainability, the quickening of the struggle for justice and peace, and the joyful celebration of life.

Historic Examples of Audacious Goals and Some for the Future

The Institute for Alternative Futures lists these examples of audacious goals and proposes some to consider for the future.

- Put a man on the moon. (John F. Kennedy, 1960)
- Prevent and eradicate polio rather than developing better iron lungs. (Jonas Salk, 1947–1955)
- Sequence the Human Genome. (James Watson, 1987)
- Democratize the automobile. (Henry Ford, 1907)
- Create a full-length animated movie. (Walt Disney, 1934)
- Build a jet that could land on runway 4-22 at LaGuardia Airport (too short for any existing passenger jet) *and* be able to fly nonstop from New York to Miami *and* be wide enough for six-abreast seating *and* have a capacity of 131 passengers *and* meet Boeing's high standards of indestructibility. (Boeing Aircraft, early 1960s, the goals that drove the development of the 727)
- Create a supercomputer that a child can use. (Steve Jobs' long-term goal for the Macintosh development team at Apple Computer)
- Mobilize a second-tier industrial power (the United States), which had manufactured only 2,141 aircraft in 1939, to quickly produce over 100,000 aircraft and put them into action in World War II. (Roosevelt's industrial mobilization produced 276,053 aircraft from 1942–1945.)

What might be a new set of goals for the U.S. federal government? For instance, by 2050, would it be possible to:

- Reduce the environmental impact of producing each unit of U.S. gross domestic product (GDP) by a factor of four?
- Make the United States energy independent in a manner that is economically beneficial, environmentally sustainable, and can be emulated around the world?
- Eliminate HIV-AIDS from the face of the Earth?
- Mobilize global cooperation to ensure access to potable water everywhere and to avoid major conflicts over water rights?

- Explore the deep oceans, creating permanent ocean stations as well as space stations?
- Reshape U.S. urban development patterns to eliminate traffic gridlock?
- Reduce health care costs while providing better care to an aging population?

These are examples of audacious goals, selected to stimulate thinking. Are some of them actually reasonable and deserving of further consideration as national goals, even though they press against the limits of what most people assume is possible? What other equally audacious goals can you propose that the government might organize around and make a difference in the world?

6

CREATING THE FUTURE THROUGH INNOVATIVE LEARNING

Sometimes we act as if innovation is a thoroughly modern notion, but human innovation has a long, global history. The Sumer culture invented a form of writing and the wheel around 3500 B.C.E. Medieval Islamic scholars were pioneers in astronomy and mathematics between 750 and 1200 C.E. The Mayan culture created an accurate solar calendar between 250 and 900 C.E. and demonstrated a sophisticated understanding of geometry in its building design. The Chinese invented written examinations around 2200 B.C.E., papermaking around 105 C.E., and moveable type in 1045 C.E.

Social innovations in how we organize human affairs are just as significant to our lives as scientific or technological innovations. A modern list of social innovations would include such diverse ideas as community colleges, public libraries, national and local parks, environmental regulations, credit cards and mortgages, Social Security, day care and elder care, product labeling, zoning regulations, and Little League baseball. Each idea was inspired by a vision of an alternative future.

Innovation completes the cycle of anticipatory learning for alternative futures. What innovations will be required to open the door to our preferred future? What solutions will we need to avoid a feared future? What incremental innovations will build on present capabilities to simply make us more effective in our expected future?

So much depends on our ability to think our way out of a world we do not want. If we cannot count on changing values and human nature quickly enough, perhaps we will be able to create social innovations that keep our worst instincts from getting ahead of our best intentions. Education is our best catalyst for equity in a world where most people struggle for the basic needs of living. The learning processes of innovation may not deliver utopia, but they do prepare us to work as if we just might come close.

INNOVATIVE LEARNING PROCESSES FOR ANY AGE

Creative thinking is not a special gift of the talented few. Businesses and organizations are finding they can be more innovative if they encourage innovative learning processes and provide a supportive environment. Schools can help students develop their capabilities to innovate new solutions by adopting these proven methodologies:

- Unlearning past successes and limitations
- Brainstorming the possibilities
- Learning across disciplines
- Simulating the choices
- Experimenting and rapid prototyping
- Observing others in action
- Continuously evaluating outcomes

Unlearning Past Successes and Limitations

The biggest obstacle to innovation is the belief that what has worked in the past will continue to do so in the future. Foresight disavows us of any false notion that everything we have learned and done in the past will be adequate. When we look at the trends, forecast their direction, or play with alternative futures in scenarios, we realize just how much change is likely. Foresight is the mental preparation to thinking differently about what we need to do to succeed.

Similarly, foresight helps us see new options when situations appear mired or the technical challenges seem too great. By scanning our environment, we can spot leverage points into an alternative future. We can see how events can open up new possibilities or a development can become a new platform for discovery.

Our past successes and failures limit our willingness to explore and entice us into comfortable channels of specialization too early. Students decide too early that they are great at math and not so good at art, or a quick study at language and not that great at sports. If we decided to educate for innovation rather than mastery, we wouldn't let this happen. We would make room in our achievement standards for exploring fields that stretch our capabilities outside our comfort zones.

Brainstorming the Possibilities

The most basic thinking methodology of innovation is brainstorming. The first rule of successful brainstorming is not to judge the ideas as they are generated. The corollary rule is that people should build on each other's ideas because something can be learned from every idea. These rules reinforce two essential truths about innovation: we are the beneficiaries of many inventions that seemed absurd at first, and every good idea can become the mother of many innovations.

Brainstorming teaches us to think in hypertext. Ideas leap off each other. Some will link to great possibilities. Even those that seem like curious diversions can validate the solutions or answers we ultimately choose.

A skilled teacher or facilitator can use brainstorming to break down conventional ways of thinking. Brainstorming encourages people to improvise on their existing mental models. Acceptable "right" answers pop out early, and then people have to reach farther from the norm to nominate as many ideas as possible. Brainstorming is also inclusive. Everyone is encouraged to contribute ideas in turn. After the ideas are prioritized for further study and development, good facilitators can affirm the contribution of any ideas not chosen by using them as a way to check the group's thinking. Are these ideas really unsuitable or simply not suitable for this situation? Would they have merit in an alternative future or situation?

Integrating Learning Across Disciplines

In the business world, innovation teams are quite often cross-functional teams with a diverse set of skills. Likewise, scientific research teams find they are more effective in addressing tough challenges when they blend knowledge and skills across disciplines. We are better able to innovate when we can draw on everything others may know.

Young children are more likely to have interdisciplinary learning experiences than high school or college students. We let education evolve into departments even though our thinking processes are not compartmentalized. Somehow, we lack sufficient imagination or coordination skills to orient higher education to the way life and work are.

In interdisciplinary learning experiences, we become collaborators and investigators in assembling the knowledge we need to address an issue. Interdisciplinary learning is typically organized around themes, issues, projects, or challenges. It fosters synthesis thinking as students borrow and blend ideas, language, and different ways of study and investigation. Once students are introduced to other disciplines, they may well discover they have an interest in studying them.

Simulating the Choices

The growing sophistication of games and simulations to model learning experiences is one of the most exciting developments in education and training. These innovative learning environments allow students to test their choices in simulated situations. Serious games truly do let students try on alternative futures and discover the consequences of their decisions. For example, educator Chris Dede and James Morrison (2004) developed an immersive multiuser virtual environment (MUVE) entitled River City to simulate water and health-related problems in a 19th-century town. Other possibilities he has proposed for taking serious games into education include:

- Teaching ethics to elementary school students through a Narnia MUVE
- Integrating mathematics, engineering, and anthropology into a Starship Enterprise MUVE
- Conducting an asthma research project that combines simulations and the Internet to engage middle school students in modeling and responding to a nationwide health problem

Another pioneer is the Massachusetts Institute of Technology's Games-to-Teach project, which creates next-generation educational media for math, science, and engineering education. One Games-to-Teach project has students using handheld PCs to work in the field as competitive teams to explore point source pollution problems. Another prototype recreates 18th-century Virginia in a three-dimensional simulation with avatars and a programmed social system. Another project lets students in environmental engineering simulate the impact that dams and highways will have.

> Educational simulations will be able to adjust themselves to the learning styles, processing speeds, and skill levels of individual users; will be able to accommodate optimized student learning teams whose members may be drawn from all parts of the world; and will be constantly upgraded to reflect new knowledge developments in a given field. The successful completion of assigned missions will serve as one form of learning assessment, and the simulation software will be intelligent enough to record the time spent on each task, to track student learning paths and completed assignments, and to use that data to determine when students have mastered the content. (Foreman, 2004)

Before long, these simulations will be available in homes and classrooms everywhere. Until that time, educators and learners can still simulate learning environments. Role-playing could be used to practice the direction-setting methodologies of strategic conversation, visioning, and goal setting. Students could pretend they are the decision makers who have to learn quickly how to define a preferred future and propose innovations to make it happen.

Experimenting and Rapid Prototyping

A desire for perfection can undermine innovation. Innovative businesses use rapid prototyping to encourage people to fail faster to get to the workable innovation sooner. Early versions are closely evaluated to improve the next version. Imagine teaching people that failing faster is a quicker way to get to quality in a classroom project. Students usually get no more than one attempt and a revision at best. By that time, they may be locked into their initial project design, and have too little time or interest to change course. With fast and early deadlines, they could test and refine their thinking before committing to a final product.

The success of Wikipedia (www.wikipedia.org) proves that open collaboration can produce surprisingly high quality work. This online knowledge resource relies on the contributions of thousands of volunteers and is designed to be edited by anyone. It has no editor or paid employees and relies on peer monitoring as its control system. Created in 2001, it now contains more than a million articles in 105 languages.

Learning through experimentation is not a free-for-all. Well-designed tests have clear objectives and working hypotheses of what learners expect to discover. They also have built-in processes for monitoring, assessing, and revising the work.

Rapid prototyping works well with team-learning projects. Until an initial work product emerges, group members have no concrete way to interact with one another to improve the product or evaluate whether they are likely to meet their objectives. Rapid prototyping may mean moving ahead without all the information, but teachers can serve as guides to close gaps in the group's knowledge if the prototype makes the state of the learning more transparent.

Experiencing the Context

To really understand the possibilities for technical or social innovations, there is no substitute for experiencing the context firsthand. Innovation expert Tom Kelley recommends taking field trips to observe "real people in real-life situations to find out what makes them tick: what confuses them, what they like, what they hate, where they have latent needs not addressed by current products and services" (Kelley, 2001, p. 6). Field investigators use the techniques of ethnography to record their observations in sufficient detail to search for environmental factors and patterns of behavior that are ripe for innovation.

If it isn't possible to go to the field, there are an amazing number of virtual field trips that recreate the live learning environment. Many museums, scientific research organizations, nature centers, and historic places have interactive websites that offer both virtual tours and opportunities to pose specific questions.

Apprenticeships and mentorships also introduce learners to real-world challenges. By engaging with a community of practice, novices have the opportunity to learn from experts. And the experts may find these fresh eyes are exactly what they need to see the possibilities for innovation they have been overlooking. The problem-solving literature is full of stories about novices seeing the solution that experts have missed.

Continuously Evaluating Outcomes

Today's optimal solution can quickly become less than satisfactory in changing conditions. New developments may make further improvements possible or entirely new solutions feasible. Innovation requires structured processes for continuously evaluating outcomes to capture the lessons learned. What worked well and what did not? This means learning teams have to candidly document both successes and failures to understand not just how an innovation works but how they learned together to create it.

In an education system that rewards innovative learning, students would be required to submit their own assessment of their learning processes with their finished product; then both the outcome and the process can be evaluated. The product may be a one-time experience for the students, but the effectiveness of their learning process will carry over into their next creative challenge.

INNOVATION PRACTICES FOR LEARNERS

Seeking Creative Environments

We need inspiring environments to spark our creativity. Unfortunately, the typical classroom, like the modern office, is designed to be more functional than inspiring. Rather than neatly lined up school desks, we need work surfaces of all sizes and types that can be configured into different arrangements for collaboration. We need bright and colorful rooms for energy, breakout rooms for teamwork, and quiet, secluded places for reflection. We need light pouring into rooms, and we need to be able to get outdoors into the light and fresh air. Our creative spaces should be visually alive with art and flooded with images and artifacts that prompt mental connections to our study and work. To invite us to play, we need props and toys that stimulate our ideas or simply invite us to relax and think freely. To move our minds and spirits, we should hear music of all types, rhythms, and intensities. We need environments that nourish us as humans to do our best thinking and work.

Our communities and lifestyles also enhance our creativity. Creative people prefer towns and cities with diverse street culture, parks and performing arts. They like places that are teeming with human and architectural diversity. They would rather be playing than watching sports. They crave authentic, active, and participatory experiences (Florida, 2002).

Cultivating Multiple Intelligences

Innovation is the only dimension of anticipatory learning that actively engages all of the multiple intelligences. No other dimension uses visual-spatial, bodily-kinesthetic, and musical intelligence as well as innovation. These intelligences are inherently connected to creative outcomes, but they also enrich our other intelligences. This may be true because they are less well developed in most people. Innovative thinking benefits from being rerouted through less familiar territory in the brain.

We can strengthen these intelligences we may not typically use. If we are not gifted in bodily-kinesthetic intelligence, body wisdom may be precisely what we need. Learning new movement skills could provide a fresh, more holistic perspective. Playing music or singing increases our expressiveness and focuses our frantic minds. Creating a visual image of our ideas can clarify our thinking and communicate it to others. These three creative intelligences also pull us inward to greater awareness and outward into activities interacting with others.

Another way to tap into multiple intelligences that may not be our special gifts is to collaborate with others who are strong where we are weak. Teams and organizations need people who are different from each other to maximize their ability to innovate. However, it is not enough to assemble a group with different capabilities. The group has to know how to make use of the gifts each person brings. A science project team may be dominated by the student with the most scientific mind without appreciating that the student with visual intelligence knows how to represent the scientific concepts, and the student with interpersonal intelligence knows exactly how best to handle the judges.

Risking Failure

Perhaps the single greatest reason we don't have more innovation is our fear of failure. We resist taking on unknown challenges, preferring to repeat what we know we can do. We fear that our innovations will be laughed at or rejected. We even fear that our innovation might succeed, ending our familiar world and thrusting us into a transformation we are unsure we desire.

When the possibility exists that unproven work could result in an F or unemployment, we think twice about how far outside the lines we are willing to color. Schools could design learning experiences that help students build their risk resilience. If students want to try something novel, their teachers could coach them in how to improve their odds for success. Innovations come from ideas that are borrowed or adapted from somewhere. Teachers can help their students connect to people with the knowledge and experience to coach them in this high-risk learning. They could help students sharpen the execution of their ideas to control for failure. And if failure cannot be avoided, they can help students accept it and understand how to capture the learning for their next attempt. Perseverance is the story of *The Little Engine That Could* and the life story of every inventor, scientist, artist, and writer who ever succeeded at something that had never been done before.

INNOVATION PRACTICES FOR LEADERS

Breaking the Hold of Bureaucracy

Whether it is bureaucracy, the status quo, or the tyranny of the urgent, a lot of stuff gets in the way of doing something new. Leaders are enablers of innovation. They make the resources available to try new solutions or create new products and processes.

Time may be the most important resource they can provide. For the teacher, it may be time away from teaching duties to develop a new curriculum. For the student, it may be flexibility in the daily schedule to work uninterrupted or to go off campus to get access to people and tools that are needed.

Expertise is another important resource leaders can offer. They do not have to be experts themselves, but they can maintain a network of contacts to connect innovators to needed expertise. This network extends into arenas that go far beyond schools to tap into alternative disciplines and communities of practice.

Education leaders also help foster innovation simply by expecting it and rewarding it. They remove the barriers that make it difficult for people to try a new approach. They expect staff and students to experiment with new ideas. Leaders endorse pilot projects and when they succeed they do more than reward the innovators. They honor the work by making sure the innovation is widely adopted.

Issuing Grand Challenges

Leaders reach into their organization's vision for the future and issue grand challenges. These are a special type of audacious goals found in direction setting. Grand challenges require people to rally their talents and focus their resources on difficult problems. They typically generate multiple innovations in tools, technologies, and processes. Here are some examples:

- The Foundation of the National Institutes of Health received $200 million from the Bill and Melinda Gates Foundation to support scientific and technological research to address Grand Challenges in Global Health. Fourteen challenges have been issued addressing vaccines, insects that transmit agents of disease, nutrition, infectious diseases, infections, and health measurement in populations.
- The U.S. National Academies of Science use grand challenges as a methodology to query scientists about the most difficult and significant challenges in their field. Grand challenges have been issued in environmental science, physics, chemistry, disaster resilience, and agricultural biotechnology.
- This grand challenge was issued within the International Society for Technology in Education: "We believe that this nation should commit itself to achieving the goal, before this decade is out, of providing a personal portable wireless computer to every student, and preparing them to use it effectively for learning in their school, their community, and their future lives" (Bull, Bull, Garofalo, & Harris, 2003).

Leaders engage their organizations and communities in defining the grand challenges embedded in their vision of a preferred future. Declaring a goal a grand challenge inspires the kind of extraordinary innovation and sustained effort it takes to do something significant. A grand challenge is so much more than this year's priorities or even a strategic goal. It may require a lifetime of learning to keep this date with our destiny.

AN OPEN QUESTION ABOUT SOCIAL INNOVATION

Every worthwhile innovation is not widely adopted. Can we learn why some ideas succeed and other perfectly good ones are neglected? Social innovations that are just good enough or "satisfice" are more likely to be legitimated. Slaughter, Naismith, and Houghton's (2004) transformative cycle is a useful tool for analyzing social legitimation. The cycle goes through four phases:

1. Breakdowns of meaning create problems to be addressed.
2. Re-conceptualization of the issue generates new possibilities.
3. Options are debated through negotiation and conflict.
4. Selective legitimation determines which innovation is chosen and implemented.

This cycle can restart if another breakdown occurs around the social innovation that was selected. Society can just as easily regress as progress in legitimating a social innovation. Our decisions are influenced by our "preferences, perceptions, actions and judgments" (Slaughter, Naismith, & Houghton, 2004).

If we could improve our learning in the conflict and negotiation phase, perhaps we would be able to more wisely choose optimal solutions. The innovations we choose to achieve our goals might not fall so far short of what we want or have so many unintended consequences. In education it seems the pendulum is forever swinging too far in one direction or another in response to the latest imperative. The problem is not our capacity to innovate. Our imagination and knowledge are more than sufficient. Our best ideas must get filtered out in the conflict and negotiation phase, perhaps because we lack shared values and a willingness to change.

℮

RECOMMENDED RESOURCES

The Future of Learning Group at the Massachusetts Institute of Technology Media Lab explores how new technologies can enable new ways of thinking, learning, and designing. The group creates new "tools to think with" and explores how these tools can help bring about change in real-world settings, such as schools, museums, and underserved communities (http://learning.media.mit.edu/index.html).

The Games-to-Teach Project, underwritten by a research grant from Microsoft iCampus, is working to develop next generation video games. The program is based in the Comparative Media Studies Department at MIT. These state-of-the-art games reach across the education disciplines from math, science, and engineering to humanities, social sciences, and language. The Games-to-Teach website is www.educationarcade.org:16080/gtt.

The International Society for Technology in Education (ISTE) is a nonprofit professional organization dedicated to providing leadership and service to improve teaching and learning by advancing the effective use of technology in K–12 education and teacher education. ISTE provides information, conferences, and guidance in incorporating computers, the Internet, and other new technologies into schools. The ISTE website is www.iste.org.

7

VISIONARY LEARNING
FOR OUR TIMES

Anticipatory learning offers a responsible approach to a future that depends on each of us having the knowledge, values, and skills needed for a sustainable way of life. The one culture that can unite us wherever we live on this planet is a learning culture.

Newspaper headlines and the images of crises streaming into our homes on television news channel prove we don't have all the time in the world to figure this out. As Csikszentmihalyi (1993) observes:

> Perhaps the most urgent task facing us is to create a new educational curriculum that will make each child aware, from the first grade on, that life in the universe is interdependent. It should be an education that trains the mind to perceive the network of causes and effects in which our actions are embedded, and trains the emotions and the imagination to respond appropriately to the consequences of those actions. . . . We bring up children to take their places in a culture that, in reality, no longer exists. The basic skills they learn have little to do with survival in the future. . . . To avoid these possibilities, it is imperative to being thinking about a truly integrative, global education that takes seriously the actual interconnectedness of causes and effects. (p. 275)

This book opened with images of the future for schools and learning that largely fit an expected future. A few images were aspiring futures that challenge the existing paradigm and contemplate the external framework of a successful future. This final chapter is an unabashedly visionary outlook for learning. Visionary futures happen when we experience a change of minds and hearts and come together to create the best future we can imagine.

FORESIGHT DEFINES LEARNING IN A PREFERRED FUTURE

Anticipatory learning questions the assumption that the official future will become reality. The official future assumes that our current successes continue to grow and our challenges are kept under control. Four key drivers could knock us off this course and make our expected future more like a feared future than a preferred future:

- The outlook for the environment anticipates global warming, endangered ecosystems and species, water shortages, and other impending limits for many natural resources.
- Issues of economic justice are dividing continents and communities along fault lines of have and have-not that leave the majority of the world's population in poverty.
- Social and cultural differences separate people into rival tribes at the brink of civil and global instability.
- Globalization is wrapping us tight in a web of interrelationships that gives new urgency to discovering our common destiny.

These are intimidating challenges. Fortunately, we are growing in our capabilities for learning our way out of crisis. The Internet gives us an unprecedented ability to collaborate at a global scale without the traditional intermediaries of national governments and multinational corporations. A tremendous amount of human knowledge now flows across institutional and geographic boundaries. This capacity for accelerated learning just might speed our transition into knowledge-based economies with the know-how to minimize waste and environmental degradation.

In our increasingly transparent world, we could call bad actors to task for their actions on a global stage. Instead, we still let renegades do too much harm before we check them, and we ought to be ashamed at how often we ignore the problems of the powerless. Even so, we are more actively engaged in learning together what to do about these challenges than at any other time in history.

EVOLVING IDENTITY THROUGH LEARNING

The Earth Charter (reprinted in Chapter 5) offers a jewel of a definition for what our identity may need to become in a preferred future: "Human development is about becoming more, not having more." The charter goes on to challenge us to live with a "sense of universal responsibility." This would require us to "eliminate discrimination in all its forms and affirm faith in the inherent dignity of all human beings."

Learning is a spiritual journey for "becoming more." To reach this stage of human development, we may have to redefine the central myth in our capitalistic identity about what constitutes quality of life. In Richard Florida's (2002) research into the creative class in America, he found that quality of life and healthy economies are linked. When we live in communities enriched with education, the arts, and livable outdoor environments, our economies become healthier as we do.

Becoming more is the purpose of lifelong learning. In our expected future, we forecast customized learning plans for students in K–12 education. In our preferred future, we will need customized learning plans throughout our lives. As our human life spans reach to 100 years and beyond, we will have many opportunities to explore alternatives for our lives. This realization should banish forever the myth that schools and universities are in the business of preparing students for one-shot careers or lives with a defined set of interests. Schools will be in the business of preparing us to negotiate different life stages to live to our fullest human potential. Ultimately this may mean getting involved in some areas that are quite surprising. We may need to put as much effort into learning how to die meaningful deaths as we have put into learning how to live purposeful lives.

SETTING DIRECTION FOR A COMPELLING VISION

Many have made a compelling case for futures studies as a priority in K–12 education to prepare students to be informed and active citizens. The success of this depends on our ability to sufficiently revitalize existing governmental structures to meet our future needs. What we may need is something more than the answers from our past.

In the preferred future envisioned by the Earth Charter, peace is defined as a "wholeness created by right relationships with oneself, other persons, other cultures, other life, Earth and the larger whole of which we are all a part." This vision strains the governing capacity of the United States, the European Union, and the United Nations. It might well be beyond the most inspired religion. No single organization can be inclusive of all that is encompassed in wholeness.

Wholeness might be possible if people are empowered across civil society to coordinate their efforts into a shared vision. Social systems are embedded in larger social systems, and success at one level influences success at the next level. We can practice meaningful direction setting wherever we are engaged in relationship with others: in classes, clubs and organizations, neighborhood groups, places of worship, local governments, and global forums. Every time we learn how to create shared vision, we gain greater capacity to move to the next level of complexity. We give lip service to living in an interconnected world, but we have much to learn about governing ourselves with a responsibility for consequences that flow in every direction.

ANTICIPATING GREATER INNOVATIONS IN LEARNING

Anticipatory learning offers many practical ideas that teachers can use to refresh the learning experience. Scanning beyond the textbook version and exercising imagination through scenarios are creative ways to engage students in learning. Defining strategic issues will give a future focus to many courses. Simulations and rapid prototyping could bring a sense of play and risk taking into learning.

Anticipatory learning will be an even more important innovation if educators choose to reorient learning from mastery of the past to preparation for the future. Reframing learning objectives in such a profound way will lead to many innovations in course design, content, and delivery. The methodologies and practices of anticipatory learning serve as a solid framework for thinking through these changes.

Anticipatory learning will make its highest contribution to a preferred future when it is used in concert with other innovations that are ahead for education. The Internet will continue to grow as an awesome tool for exploration. Students could learn in virtual communities across cultures to exercise their shared identities as citizens of the world. They could integrate learning across disciplines by actually communicating with the field scientists who are working to preserve our biosphere, for example.

Many schools are certain to take on new forms in the future as we unlearn past successes and limitations. The early indicators of an era of greater innovation can be found in charter and magnet schools today. Today they are the special cases, but they have shown us what a compelling vision can do for learning.

The grand challenge for schools is to empower students to contribute actively to a preferred future. We assume that the necessary breakthroughs can only spring from the minds of research scientists, engineers, and government leaders. They could just as easily be in the minds of students who can imagine a different world and learn their way into it.

A LEARNING CULTURE THAT UNIFIES ACROSS TIME

We live in a time of split-second opportunities and threats. We could just as easily fall into a feared future as stay on track for an expected future. For a preferred future, we need to do much better than simply stay in step with rapid technological and evolutionary advances. Anticipatory learning gives us the learning and skills to shape our future in complex and interdependent times.

We owe our ancestors deep gratitude for the knowledge they have given us. We owe our descendents the anticipatory learning that keeps the possibilities for their potential alive. A preferred future takes many lifetimes of inspired learning.

REFERENCES

Ann Arbor Public Schools. (2005). *Mission, core values and strategic goals.* Retrieved March 1, 2005, from http://www.aaps.k12.mi.us/aaps.about/mission_values_goals.

Bell, Wendell. (2002). Making people responsible: the possible, the probable, and the preferable. In James Dator (Ed.), *Advancing futures, futures studies in higher education.* Westport, CT: Praeger.

Bishop, Peter. (2002). Social change and futures practice. In James Dator (Ed.), *Advancing futures, futures studies in higher education.* Westport, CT: Praeger.

Bleedorn, Bernice (2003). *An education track for creativity and other quality thinking processes.* Lanham, MD: Scarecrow Press.

Botkin, James, Elmandjra, Mahdi, & Malitza, Mircea. (1979). *No limits to learning: Bridging the human gap.* Oxford: Pergamon Press.

Bull, Glen, Bull, Gina, Garofalo, Joe, & Harris, Judi. (2003). *Grand challenges: Preparing for the technological tipping point.* Retrieved October 11, 2004, from http://curry.edschool.virginia.edu/class/edlf/589-18/tipping.doc.

Creating Preferred Futures. (2005). *Rationale.* Retrieved March 25, 2005, from http://.cpfonline.org/cpf/rationale.php.

Csikszentmihalyi, Mihaly. (1993). *The evolving self: A psychology for the third millennium.* New York: HarperCollins.

Dator, James A. (Ed.). (2002). *Advancing futures, futures studies in higher education.* Westport, CT: Praeger.

Dede, Chris, & Morrison, James. (2004, October/November). The future of learning technologies: An interview with Chris Dede. *Innovate Journal of Online Education, 1*(1). Retrieved September 22, 2004, from www.innovateonline.info/index.php.

Dickinson, Dee. (2002). Learning through many kind of intelligences. *New Horizons for Learning*. Retrieved July 28, 2004, from www.newhorizons.org.

Earth Charter Organization (2005). *The earth charter initiative*. Retrieved February 3, 2005, from http://www.earthcharter.org/.

Emmerling, Robert J., & Goleman, Daniel. (2003). Emotional Intelligence: Issues and Common Misunderstandings. *Issues in Emotional Intelligence*. Retrieved July 28, 2004, from www.eiconsortium.org/index.html.

Florida, Richard. (2002). *The rise of the creative class*. New York: Basic Books.

Foreman, Joel. (2004, October/November). Video game studies and the emerging instructional revolution. *Innovate Journal of Online Education, 1*(1). Retrieved September 22, 2004, from www.innovateonline.info/index.php.

Gardner, Howard. (2004). *Changing minds: The art and science of changing our own and other people's minds*. Boston, MA: Harvard Business School Press.

Gergen, J. Kenneth. (1991). *The saturated self: Dilemmas of identity in contemporary life*. New York: BasicBooks.

Gidley, Jennifer. (2004). Futures/foresight in education at primary and secondary levels: A literature review and research task analysis. In *Futures in Education, Principles Practice and Potential*. Melbourne: Swinburne Press.

Goleman, Daniel, Boyatzis, Richard, & McKee, Annie. (2002). *Primal leadership: Realizing the power of emotional intelligence*. Boston: Harvard Business School Press.

Green, Hardy. (2004, October 11). Building on the Past. *Newsweek*.

Hicks, David. (2003). A futures perspective: Lessons from the school room. *Journal of Futures Studies, 7*(3), 55–64.

Hirsch, Sandra Krebs, & Kummerow, Jean M. (1987). *Introduction to type in organizational setting*. Palo Alto, CA: Consulting Psychologisst Press.

Hodgins, Wayne. (2000). Into the future: A vision paper for the American Society of Training and Development and the National Governors Association. Retrieved November 11, 2004, from www.learnativity.com/into_the_future2000.html.

Horn, Raymond A., Jr. (2004, April/May). Building capacity for the development of a critical democratic citizenry through the redefinition of education. *World Futures, The Journal of General Evolution, 60*(3), 169–182.

Inayatullah, Sohail. (2000). *Questioning the future*. Taipei: Tamkang University.

Inayatullah, Sohail. (2003, February). Teaching futures studies from strategy to transformative change. *Journal of Futures Studies, 3*, 35–40.

Isaacs, William. (1999). *Dialogue and the art of thinking together*. New York: Doubleday.

Jenks, C. Lynn. (2004, April/May). Missing links in the public school curriculum: Four dimensions for change. *World Futures, The Journal of General Evolution, 60*(3), 195–216.

Jenlink, Patrick M. (2004, April/May). Education and the evolution of society; Also education, social creativity and the evolution of society; Also reflections: Education and our shared future. *World Futures, The Journal of General Evolution, 60*(3), 161–167.

Johnson, David W., & Johnson, Frank P. (1997). *Joining together, group theory & group skills*. Boston, MA: Allyn & Bacon.

Kelley, Tom. (2001). *The art of innovation*. New York: Currency/Doubleday.

Lawley, James, & Tompkins, Penny. (2002). *Metaphors in mind: Transformation through symbolic modeling*. London: Developing Company Press.

Montgomery County Public Schools. (2005). *Mission and core values*. Retrieved March 1, 2005, from http://www.mcps.K12.md.us./departments/student services/mission.shtm.

National Institue of Mental Health. (2005). *Treatment of children with mental disorders*. Retrieved March 25, 2005, from http://www.nimh.nih.gov/publicat/childqa.cfm.

North Central Regional Education Laboratory. *Develop a clear, educationally focused vision*. Retrieved August 10, 2004, from www.ncrel.org/sdrs/areas/issues/educatrs/leadrshp/le1clear.htm.

Olson, Robert, & Dighe, Atul. (2001). *Exploring the future: Seven strategic conversations that could transform your association*. Washington, DC: American Society of Association Executives.

Ontario Ministry of Education. (2004). *Progress report: OECD "Teaching as a Profession" project*. Toronto, ON: International Schooling for Tomorrow Forum.

Organisation for Economic Co-operation and Development (OECD). (2001). *Schooling for tomorrow: What schools for the future?* Paris: Centre for Educational Research & Innovation.

Rubin, Anita. (2002). Giving images a chance: images of the future as a tool of sociology. In James Dator (Ed.)., *Advancing futures, futures studies in higher education*. Westport, CT: Praeger.

Senge, Peter M. (1990). *The fifth discipline: The art and practice of the learning organization*. New York: Currency/Doubleday.

Senge, Peter, Scharmer, C. Otto, Jaworski, Joseph, & Flowers, Betty Sue. (2004). *Presence: Human purpose and the field of the future*. Cambridge, MA: Society of Organizational Learning.

Simmons, Annette. (2002). *The story factor: Inspiration, influence and persuasion through the art of storytelling*. New York: Perseus.

Slaughter, Richard. (1994). From fatalism to foresight—Educating for the early 21st century. Melbourne: Australian Council for Educational Administration.

Slaughter, Richard. (2003). Interview on skills for the future. *British Broadcasting Corporation*. Retrieved November 11, 2004, from www.bbc.co.uk/worldservice/ sci_tech/features/essentialguide/download/education/prog1.rtf.

Slaughter, Richard A., Naismith, Luke, & Houghton, Neil. (2004). *The transformative cycle*. Melbourne: Swinburne University, Australian Foresight Institute.

Toffler, Alvin. (1970/1984). *Future shock*. New York: Bantam.

van Aalst, Hans F. (2001). The driving forces for schooling tomorrow: Insights from studies in four countries. In Organization for Economic Cooperation and Development (Ed.), *Schooling for tomorrow: What schools for the future* (pp. 157–176). Paris: Centre for Educational Research & Innovation.

Virginia Beach City Public Schools. (2005). *Vision Statement, mission statement and core values*. retrieved March 1, 2005, from http://www.vbschools.com/ mission%5Fcore.html.

World Transhumanism Association. (2005). *Declaration*. Retrieved March 20, 2005, from http://transhumanism.org/index.php/WTA/declaration.

ABOUT THE AUTHOR

Marsha Lynne Rhea, senior futurist with the Institute for Alternative Futures (IAF), specializes in helping nonprofits and other collaborative organizations create their preferred future. She blends a futurist's skills and perspective with more than 20 years experience as a nonprofit executive.

IAF, based in Alexandria, Va., has a 28-year track record of guiding associations, corporations, and governments to align their future with their highest aspirations. Rhea has been a speaker and consultant for clients in education, health care, business, and the environment. She works with boards and senior leadership teams to define the vision and strategies to transform their organizations. As a futurist, she gets to work with people who want to make their greatest contribution to the future. Her work requires her to learn at the leading edge of different fields and emerging issues.

Prior to joining IAF in January 2001, Rhea held executive leadership positions with the American Society of Association Executives (ASAE), the National Recycling Coalition, and the American Subcontractors Association. She began her association career working for the Alabama and Georgia school board associations and serving as editor of a national newspaper for the Arthritis Foundation. She worked as a newspaper reporter for the *Florida Times-Union* and the *Montgomery Advertiser*, where she covered education.

Rhea earned a master's degree in nonprofit management from George Mason University and an undergraduate degree from Georgetown College in Kentucky. Exemplifying her commitment to lifelong learning, she completed the 6-year Institute of Organization Management program of the U.S. Chamber of Commerce and earned the certified association executive designation from ASAE.